THE LUCID DREAM MANIFESTO

THE LUCID DREAM MANIFESTO

✦

Reprint Of: Lucid Dreams, Dreams and Sleep: Theoretical Constructions, 1974

Daniel Oldis

iUniverse, Inc.
New York Lincoln Shanghai

THE LUCID DREAM MANIFESTO
Reprint Of: Lucid Dreams, Dreams and Sleep: Theoretical Constructions, 1974

iUniverse books may be ordered through booksellers or by contacting:

iUniverse
2021 Pine Lake Road, Suite 100
Lincoln, NE 68512
www.iuniverse.com
1-800-Authors (1-800-288-4677)

Published as Lucid Dreams, Dreams and Sleep: Theoretical Constructions
University of South Dakota Media Press, 1974

ISBN-13: 978-0-595-39539-2
ISBN-10: 0-595-39539-2

Printed in the United States of America

Contents

AUTHOR'S PREFACE TO THE 2006 PRINTING

In the late sixties and early seventies, researchers investigating the unique phenomenon now widely known as "lucid dreaming" were operating on the fringe of the fringe of science. Dick McLeester's 1976 dream bibliography, *Welcome to the Magic Theatre: A Handbook for Exploring Dreams,* cites only a handful of publications relating to the topic, this treatise being one of them. Today, a Web search for "lucid dreaming" or "lucid dreams" returns over one million results. Indeed, things have come a long way for this exciting subject.

At the time I was writing this book, dream studies were in a state of transition, moving further away from psychoanalytic and Gestalt interpretations toward cognitive and physiological explanations. In a few short years of my writing this manuscript, J. Allan Hobson of Harvard would permanently reshape the dream landscape with his activation-synthesis theory. Dreams lost their teleology, their purposeful role in the mental development of the individual and become best-fit fleeting creations of the brain making sense of random excitations. The dreamer becomes a harried screenwriter trying to construct a script out of bad material.

Lucid dreams, however, did not suffer from this shift in perspective. The ability to be aware in your dream that you are dreaming has little dependency on the underlying function of dreaming (or sleeping). Perhaps the meaninglessness of normal dreams gives impetus to the desire to give them meaning through lucid conscious observation and control. In fact, the study and practice of lucid dreaming may be said to have become the number one dream topic in contemporary discussions and conferences.

This reprint of my original text is intended for readers and students interested in the history of this topic and some of its early theoretical underpinnings. The manuscript also offers some fairly far-fetched (but cool) biochemical theories of sleep and dreams that anticipated Hobson but which are almost assuredly wrong. Read at your own risk.

Techniques for achieving lucidity in dreams are widely disseminated and can be found on the Web or in bookstores. The reader is advised to seek these out rather than relying on my own experiments that are presented in this book.

While my crude experiments played a role in inciting other, more reliable, techniques, they are extremely unscientific and anecdotal.

I would like to offer belated thanks to individuals that reviewed or excerpted my work or gave me other encouragement back then when I was a young graduate student in English and broke: Ann Faraday, Dick McLeester, Carrol McLaughlin, Robert L. Van de Castle, Celia Green, Stephen Laberge, Steve Blum, Jan Berkhout, and my friends and family for giving me cash and keeping me in cigars.

Sweet (and lucid) dreams to all of you.

PREFACE:
THE DREAM REVOLUTION

Indeed, there is no dream revolution, never was, unless of course one considers the cathartic revelations of Freud or ocular discoveries of Kleitman to be revolutions. Surely, they were monumental and prolific but a revolution indicates change and connotes conquest; neither Freud nor Kleitman changed dreams, much less conquered them. They studied, interpreted and recorded these mental dramas but remained observers, analytical technicians. Let us call them insurrectionists, then, brilliant insurrectionists but insurrectionists at best.

The true revolutionaries were men with obscure names like Fox and van Eeden—rebels altering the nature of dreams and conquering their substance. Yet why then, one may ask, if these men were changing the structure of man's most arcane and cryptic experience were they relatively unnoticed and unknown until but recently and their endeavors ignored or dissipated into esoteric genre and extreme regions of a scientific climate? Perhaps it is because like many revolutionaries they did not fully understand the nature of that which they were changing or the direction of the change. In the manner of the misanthrope in an assassination attempt, who neither understands his actions or the forces that precipitated them, the potential for change will be misdirected, misinterpreted or forgotten.

It is with this paper that I hope to lend direction and meaning to the accounts of such men; to elucidate the nature of the revolutionary milieu (dreams and sleep); and to provide a viable proposal for the movement towards change in the dream theory and operational use.

This is not intended as a treatise or manifesto for a dream revolution. Rather, it is an offering: an offering of theoretical constructions and experimental observations. If it is taken as a valuable approach and reasoned determination, then fine; if it is found wanting in support or logical consequence, then surely science will be nonetheless. My background is infinitesimal to nonexistent; my research much too cursory in nature; my experimental devices parochial. Yet here it is and if as it is said, the thought precedes the act, then I think change, I think revolution.

PART I:
INTRODUCTION TO LUCID DREAMS

It is an unfortunate concomitant of scientific temperament that it sees to its own. Ideas brought forth into this world of aesthetic or metaphysical procreation assume positions tantamount to fourth cousins thrice removed in the scientist's scheme of value. Even if by matrimony to one of the treasured methods they should be embraced as "family", their arrival will always be stigmatized with questionable beginnings.

Metaphorical case in point: "lucid dreams"—victims of scientific indifference for over fifty years due to an unpropitious nurture in the occult. Not that the psychic species of endeavor are either inferior or provincial but that in the particular instance of "lucid dreams" the psychologically salutary aspects of the phenomenon might have found facilitation had the established orders of mental science given it the time of day.

Speaking anecdotic, it all started with an article appearing in *Proceedings of the Society for Psychical Research* (July 1913) by a Dr. F. van Eeden concerning a particular type of dream that he termed "lucid"; or a dream in which one is aware in the dream that he is indeed dreaming. This was followed seven years later by two articles published in the *Occult Review* (1920) by a man named Oliver Fox; articles dealing with a phenomenon of mind-body separation later termed "astral projection," which was a direct result of a unique dream experience called by Mr. Fox a "dream of knowledge" or, if you will, a lucid dream. Right here with these two accounts the psychological savants of Europe and America should have jumped on "lucid dream" and "dream of knowledge" as important aspects of altered consciousness. Yet the directional current of science at the time was toward the experimental and observational techniques such as psychoanalysis and away from the subjective, spiritually-pigmented accounts of "psychics." In short, they didn't read them.

With these not so auspicious beginnings, lucid dreams continued to be classi-fied in the Para-psychological phylum; and with the subsequent publishing of Sylvian Muldoon's *The Projection of the Astral Body* (1929) and Fox's *Astral Pro-jection: A Record of Out of Body Experiences* (1962 in America) lucid dreams became synonymous with mind-body separation. This relationship found some redefinition, however, in J.H.M. Whiteman's *The Mystical Life* (1961) wherein the point of departure between a lucid dream and astral projections was made dependent on certain psychological criteria. Today lucid dreams can by found in sundry psychic anthologies such as Susy Smith's *Out of the Body Experiences* in the same general context as astral projection.

Yet the relegation of lucid dreams by the experimental communities of psy-chophysics could not continue indefinitely. In the late sixties two individuals at leading university centers liberated the phenomenon from its cul-de-sac. In 1968 Celia Green, director of the Institute of Psychophysical Research at Oxford, pub-lished a book titled appropriately *Lucid Dreams*; giving lucid dream study a direc-tion and significance long overdue. By distinguishing lucid dreams from astral experience. Miss Green opened the way for scientific methodology; and by orchestrating various aspects and causal agents of the event along with suggesting such experimental techniques as EEG recordings of "lucidity," she gave it the necessary "respectability" for its scientific "coming out." Not long after, Charles Tart included lucid dreams in his *Altered States of Consciousness: A Book of Read-ings* (1969) along with LSD experience and alpha meditation; thereby officially acknowledging them as natural rather than supernatural occurrences.

In this past decade, then, while lucid dreams have not altogether been estranged from their psychic kinship they have caught the eye, so to speak, of supercilious academicians over the world.

Capitulation is in order. Surely it cannot be expected of psychologists and related disciplinarians to investigate and survey all reported extra-sensory origi-nating events. If that were so who could be expected to inspect all psychologically originating events—hardly the occultists. With only so many personnel, money and time the experimental and behavioral sciences can be anticipated to do no more than care for their own first. And yet as an incidental and passé note it might be mentioned that had mental illness, which originally was associated with supernatural demon possession, been confined to that realm because of its begin-nings, the shape and form of contemporary life would be considerably retarded.

With these digressive introductions dispelled, it is now necessary to define lucid dreams in greater detail and lend meaning to their occurrence. As men-tioned before lucid dreams are, as reported consensus has it, a unique dream experience which evolves from an ordinary dream and commences when the dreamer realizes for one reason or another that he is dreaming and that the events happening around him are images of his own creation. At first glance this might not seem to be such a big deal: "So what, so I know in a dream that I 'm dreaming, now what?" The response is: "So what, so you can consciously inspect your own experiential and genetic memory processes; observe the inner elaboration and manifestations of your own psyche weave into a contrapuntal hallucinatory scheme; so you are a veritable god in a universe of your own making; you can do anything, go anywhere, anytime in a dream world that can offer the "real" impressions and senses of waking life: What do you do?" The simple significance of lucid dreams is that they are dreams, but dreams wherein one is aware of that fact, aware that in this endogenous environment there are no limits, no inhibitions, no fears; in fact practically no perimeters to his volition. The implications of this mere fact of awareness or lucidity are staggering, the psychological ramifications cataclysmic. What does a person do when the restrictive forces of physics and society are obliterated, when he can fly to an imaginative moon, walk through a wall, or make love to a surrogate princess?

It is to this determination of lucidity, this dream awareness that accounts, articles and books have been dedicated; this small point of knowledge that is becoming recognized by some mental pundits as a point capable of pivoting emotional theory. And yet despite this potential, despite this growing interest, there have been no published accounts attempting either to formulate a general theory on sleep and dreams utilizing and incorporating lucid dreams or provide a physiological and psychological preface for their existence. Neither has there been, other than Green's observations of interest initiated lucidity, a systematic attempt to experimentally induce lucid dreams in normal individuals using classical psychological techniques.

This, of course, is the self-appointed task of my paper; to propose a general theory consistent with lucid dreams, a possible basis for their occurrence, and methods by which they can be evoked. It will, however, be necessary first to offer a cursory outline of the history of lucid dreams; discuss various aspects germane to the experience, present selections from records of lucid adventurers pertaining to these aspects; include my own accounts in this presentation; and determine the ability or inability of conventional and contemporary dream theories to absorb or explain lucid dreams and various evidential findings.

NOTES ON PART I

1. Since the original draft of this paper, it has been discovered that other dream researchers have investigated the possibility of using interest initiation as a method of learning lucid dreaming. Patricia Garfield in *Creative Dreaming*. 1978 and Ann Faraday in *The Dream Game*, 1975, both suggest reading and dream diaries as useful aids in developing lucidity. Greg Sparrow in *The Sundance Community Dream Journal*, 1976, prescribes interest and meditation as possible lucid initiators.

PART II:
HISTORY OF LUCID
DREAMS

To regress briefly, Dr. van Eeden published the first recorded testimonial of extended lucid dream experiences in 1913; Oliver Fox seven years later. Van Eeden, in a period between 1898 and the writing of his article, experienced and recorded 352 dreams of which he classified as "lucid." While Fox never specified, the indications from his writings suggest that he at least equaled or exceeded that number.

During this time period there were also two other persons, Mrs. Arnold Forster (1921) and Y. Delage (1919), who reported published events of dream lucidity. Yet neither of their accounts possessed the volume or scope of van Eeden's or Fox's. Their encounters with lucid dreams were either too few or ill-defined to merit an ascendant position in lucid history.

Of course Muldoon (1929) has already been discussed in respect to the misapprehended equation of lucid dreams and astral projection. With Muldoon it is difficult to discriminate between the point of mental dream and mental separation. Yet despite this penchant toward the para-normal and disregarding my own fragmentary knowledge of his writings, it does seem within the confines of anthological propriety to include him as a prominent figure in the tradition of lucid dreams—if for no other reason than his influence on Oliver Fox and others coming later.

It was not until the 1960's that the next transcribed phenomena of lucid dreams were made available to the world of extraordinary aficionados. I owe my knowledge of these publications as well as those of Delage and Arnold Forster to Miss Green's book on the subject. Accordingly it was discovered that P.D. Ouspensky (1960), J.H.M. Whiteman (1961), and the Marquis d'Hervey Saint-Denys (1964) all recorded dreams of the lucid variety—Ouspensky for the reason of consciously observing the sequence and development of ordinary dreams rather that probing the unique potentials of the lucid occasion itself.

5

At this point Green and Tart enter the lucid historical arena as earlier introduced with their efforts at organizational definition and initiation of the lucid condition into analytical science; although neither had any pronounced personal association with it to draw upon.

It is here where I place my own lucid experiences spanning a recorded five year period from 1969 to the date of this writing and consisting of over fifty extended lucid dreams. Having read at the onset only Fox's Astral Projection it was understandable that my original approach, as denoted by the title of my own journal, "Experiments in Astral Projection, March 1, 1969," was one tending toward the extra-sensory. However, as the occurrences of lucid dreams became more frequent and prolonged as well as making the discovery that most people questioned responded affirmatively to at least ephemeral lucid realizations (in most cases during nightmares), I began to question the psychic nature of the phenomenon. Consequently, for a period of over two years the salient activity of my lucid dream experience was to ascertain whether it was an out-of-body or endogenous mental exercise.

Primarily I conducted in-dream experiments such as viewing a clock during the lucid period and then checking it upon awakening; or visiting a friend's house in the dream and attempting to observe events and such for later verification. On the whole the experiments were inconclusive; but as the function of this paper proscribes psychic-psychological argumentation my investigation into the question will be postponed until the last section on speculative considerations. Also rather than present a sequential diary of my lucid ad-ventures a la Fox, I will reserve individual dream accounts for their respective categorical contributions.

If this history of lucid dreams seems somewhat impoverished it is possibly because of two reasons: first, only published or recorded lucid events have been included here and, as will be shown later, the existence of lucidity is considerably more prevalent than documentation would indicate; and also by reason of its previously discussed para-psychological heritage, preventing scientific support and promulgation.

NOTES ON PART II

1. A recent addition to the history of "dreams of knowledge" comes from a series of "books written "by a UCLA, graduate student and its: inclusion here causes some difficulty. First, there is some uncertainty as to whom. to credit with the lucid occurrences—Carlos Castaneda or his friend Don Juan; and second, it is somewhat difficult to determine if the "dreaming" discussed in such books as *A Separate Reality, Journey to Ixtlan,* and *Tales of Power* is intended to "be an imaginative or mystical occasion. Indeed, whether anthropological or fictional, Castaneda's writing is significant in that it evinces a clear case for the possibilities of learning and practicing lucid dreaming; and it offers, a fascinating look at the potentials, and adventures awaiting an "aware" dreamer,

PART III:
THE NATURE OF LUCID DREAMS AND IMPLICATIONS FOR SLEEP AND DREAM THEORY

The essence of lucid dreams has already been presented—a dream of awareness of ones own dreaming state (such awareness will be shown later to be a natural extension of normal dream thought). However, this general definition and the presence of enormous volitional potential do not completely satisfy the descriptive requirements of the dreams. Here, then, an attempt will be made to illustrate various attributes prior to and within the lucid condition and discuss what implication they might have for dream theory.

Initially one would be inclined to ask: "How does a person find out he's dreaming; what initiates the lucid dream?" This is a question which has been dealt with by practically all lucid dreamers and which occupies a considerable part of both this paper and the past five years of my association with the experience. While later I will offer methods by which lucid dreams can be learned and acquired by anyone, here the emphasis will be on the spontaneous arousal of lucidity in documented and my own cases.

Celia Green posits four natural processes by which lucid dreams occur. They are: 1. emotional stress within a dream; 2. recognition of incongruity within a dream; 3. lucidity arising from the initiation of analytical thought; 4. recognition of the dream-like quality of the experience.

Oliver Fox considers the arousal of a "critical faculty" as a necessary preliminary for a lucid dream. This "critical faculty" can be inferred from Fox to be some sort of propensity toward critical inspection of the dream environment as to its credibility. Apparently Fox believes that this faculty exists prior to the particular dream event in different levels but that the dream event can serve as a catalyst for its arousal. This catalyst would work in similar ways to Green's .processes.

As for myself, I will introduce later reasoning to support the conception that all of Green's processes are but a single psychological tributary of a continuing mental process of dream stimuli and reasoned response. Yet, for purposes of logical and ordered composition, it will do for now to observe each of these processes as disparate mental functions.

1. Emotional stress within a dream—primarily recurrent dreams and nightmares. The person realizes that the situation that he is in has happened before in dreams so this present situation must also be a nightmare or dream. An example from Green:

> From early childhood until I was about 45 I had recurring dreams, and in my sleep I used to find myself saying, 'of course I know, I've had it many times before1 and if it was a nice one I would let it run on, and if nasty I could switch it off and wake up." Another:
> "Those dreams in which I am aware that I am dreaming are of two kinds. Both are of an unpleasant nature. The first type is a recurrent nightmare, now not so common as it was when I was about 12, when it was very frequent. In this nightmare, I am searching for something incredibly small that it is vital that I find before someone else, who, though never named, is in some way evil. Having now had this dream some dozens of times, even in my dreaming I realize both that I am dreaming, and that I have dreamt it before.

My own case of lucidity arising from a recurrent nightmare is one where I dream I am in an elevator and it begins to fall. I become frightened and then realize that this same thing has happened many times before in what turned out to be nothing more than nightmares. Thus this too must be just a dream since it is like the others. Here most people would decide to wake but I continue the awareness into a lucid dream and change the scene before the elevator crashes.

2. Recognition of incongruity, or the determination that the dream objects or scenes are incongruous in relation to one another. It must be emphasized that in this instance it is not the realization of the distortion of the dream compared to waking life as all varieties of distortion and incongruity in relation to waking life can occur without lucid determination; but rather a violation of in-dream "realities" and relationships. An example from Fox's own accounts might help to clarify:

> I dreamed that I was standing on the pavement outside my home. The sun was rising behind the Roman wall. Now the pavement was not of the ordinary type, but consisted of small, bluish-gray rectangular stones with their long sides at right-angles to the white curb. I was about to enter the house when, on glancing casually at these stones, my attention became riveted by a passing strange phenomenon, so extraordinary that I could not believe my eyes—they had seemingly all changed their position in the night, and the long sides were now parallel to the curb! Then the solution flashed upon me: though this glorious summer morning seemed as real as real could be, I was dreaming!

Here the stones' positions in one part of the dream were incongruous to their positions in another part. It is not important what the position of the stones was in real life or even if there were stones, but that one segment of the same dream violated another segment and a relationship already established.

3. Lucidity arising from the initiation of analytical thought. Green defines this as: "lucidity may arise when the dream situation is of such a kind that, if it happened in waking life, it would initiate a train of analytical or critical thought in the subjects mind." She gives this instance of lucid attainment by analytical thought:

> This dream took place on the upper floor of a large, rather atmospheric mansion. I went along the corridor to another room and Began to talk in the air. After a little, words I had said began to echo back to me from the walls and corners of the room. This began to seem unnatural, as isolated words were picked out of what I said and echoed repeatedly. Also the same word was echoed back from different angles. I became uneasy and left the room before I became more so. As I walked back along the corridor I wondered whether such an odd sort of echo could be naturally caused. At this point I realized that I was dreaming.

In this case the subject developed a critical attitude toward the echoes and analytically determined (implicitly) that he must be dreaming. From my own files:

> I was walking in a dream with a friend down the sidewalk. I was telling him how great it was to see him after so long. He said, "It's nice to be back and thanks for going to so much trouble to pick me up at the train station." I then noticed that I didn't remember picking him up or for that matter how we happened to be walking together. Next it dawned on me that we didn't even have a train station in my town. This led to the rationalization that I must be dreaming the whole thing.

While as shown here analytical thought processes can lead to lucid dreams, they do not always do so. Later, examples will be given of subjects critically inspecting the dream environment and determining that they are not dreaming but awake. As a somewhat ironic note along these lines; once in a dream I was explaining this exact thing to a fellow student: that in order to have a "dream of knowledge" he must first analyze his surroundings and determine if they were logical. And the entire time I was relating this I never once realized that this whole conversation was itself a dream1

The fourth process of Green's: recognition of dreamlike quality of the experience is a spontaneous realization of the dream condition without preliminary analytical thought. The person suddenly recognizes that the situation is dreamlike. Here are her examples from retrieved reports:

> I was, I thought, standing in my study; but I observed that the furniture had not its usual distinctness—that everything was blurred and somehow evaded a direct gaze. It struck me that this must be because I was dreaming.

> In an ordinary dream I was trying to get on a bus that I was chasing along the road, dodging in and out of traffic and holding a ribbon that connected me to the bus. This ribbon seemed to be elastic and I noticed with annoyance that it was elongating and I was falling behind. Then I realized that I was dreaming and did not need to chase the bus or even to dodge the traffic. So I stopped running and stood still in the road—the traffic vanished as I did so.

And yet upon inspection it appears that a rapid logical sequence has indeed preceded the determination—critical observation in the first case, recognition of incongruity in the second (of the ribbon becoming elongated). Apparently the lack of an obvious train of thought rests not within the dream but with the dream recall and its patented memory deficiencies. Therefore, it is likely that this fourth process is similar to the second or third but with forgotten logical development upon awakening.

Once this dream determination of lucidity is made by whatever process there remains two alternatives: to wake up or remain in the dream. Most common encounters with lucidity and awareness result in awakening as they predominantly evolve from nightmares and the sleeper wishes to awake from the unpleasant situation; although this is the prerogative of the dreamer in most instances, and he has the ability, if he wishes, to continue the hallucinatory state. This continuity of the dream perceptual scene might, however, require a certain amount of volition or concentration as there does seem to be at times a tendency to wake up. Fox describes this tendency or feeling as "dual consciousness": a struggle for dominance between the external sensory impressions upon the sleeper and the internal dream impulses. I also have experienced the sensation of being both in the dream world and lying on a bed of the real world simultaneously. (The physiological reasons for this "dual consciousness" will be discussed in the section the on cortical/reticular/pons relationship during sleep and dreams.) Yet at most times mere desire to remain dreaming and direction of attention on dream images will result in the subsidence of the external impressions and accentuation of the imaginary drama.

When the dream and lucidity are within a well defined milieu the subject enters an emotional state of ineffable freedom and omnipotence. Yet this state and the degree of voluntary control of the dream range from passive awareness and observation of dream sequence to complete control of the perceptual body, dream objects, and entire scene. Each of these will be investigated in turn.

An example of passive inspection exists in my own diary.

> I was standing talking to a schoolmate across from the school we were attending. Suddenly the entire school building burst into flames. I said to him that things just don't catch fire that quickly and that the only answer for it was that we were both in a dream of mine. He suggested that if it were a dream, why didn't I put it out by effort of will or fly to the fire station and get help. I tried but could do neither, only stand and watch.

To annotate, it will be noted that possibly this failure on my part to direct my dream body or the dream objects might be attributed to an innate desire on the part of all students since elementary age to see the school burn down (i.e. "I saw the glory of the burning of the school, etc.") In effect, maybe my effort of will was no effort at all.

Normally in lucid dreams the easiest thing to control is the dream perpetual body or the "I" in a dream. Almost all habitual lucid dreamers find flying to be one of the simplest tasks of all; albeit at times it might be difficult to determine the direction or elevation once in the air. Fox defines this uncontrolled levitation as "stirring" and offers a word of caution about its use in the sense that one might be carried off into space. Perhaps Mr. Fox has forgotten that should this event arise all one would have to do is awaken.

The method by which flying is performed in lucid dreams varies. Green offers two of them from subject recall:

As I greatly wished to reach the summit of this beautiful building, I decided to levitate and made the slight paddling motions, which I have hitherto found necessary, at the same time leaning backwards as though about to float on water.

My usual method of aerial progression in lucid dreams was a bounding motion from the earth upwards, over the tops of houses and trees and then back to earth and another bound and so on.

In my own lucid states I usually fly either by jumping off buildings and such horizontally or by leaping up from the ground, forming a horizontal position and then by concentration slowly rising upwards.

Most probably it makes no difference what method is used to fly but instead what method the dreamer believes is necessary to fly as it is imagination, not physics with which we are dealing here.

A second rather popular function of perceptual body control is walking through walls—quite a feeling in its own right. And yet walking through walls might instead be more of a scene control event: willing the dream scene to change from one side to what it would be expected to be like on the other side of the wall.

Not all lucid travelers report manipulation of dream objects. And of those that do the extent of manipulation and responsiveness of the dream object vary greatly. Oliver Fox writes, "I could also do some intriguing little tricks at will, such as moving objects without visible contact, and molding the plastic matter into new forms."

Subject B, of Green's observations reports on his attempt at image control:

Dreaming that I was walking along a road I thought I would like to have an apple. I saw a patch on the road ahead and thought, 'By the time I reach that it will be an apple.1 Before reaching it, I found I had another apple in my hand. I examined it thinking, 'Quite a credible imitation of an apple!

And another:

I considered what I was wearing and thought I would like a doublet and hose so made them appear beside me and put them on. Saw someone watching the materialization of the clothes with some surprise and thought they had no idea how easy it really was in a dream.

I have found that in lucid dreams the control factor is inversely proportional to the objects relative size if it were real. For example, I find opening doors without touching them fairly easy with an effort of will. However, lifting the dream facsimile of a car by mental command requires enormous concentration and is at most times futile. This same relationship holds true for image manifestation from scratch. I can make little things appear quite easily but large objects are considerable more difficult to materialize.

A total dream scene change is the hardest to achieve. It is rarely an instantaneous transformation. Miss Green considers dream traveling to be the usual method for environmental change: "Few, if any, cases are on record of a subject consciously selecting the environment in which he would like to find himself and simply willing his present dream environment to change into it. Subjects may decide that they wish to travel to a certain place and, after some kind of simulated spatial displacement, find themselves where they wish to be."

One case reported by subject D of Green's studies reveals a situation of image metamorphosis as a method of scene alteration:

> I decided that a glass-house at Kew Gardens would look better than my surroundings, for that reason I concentrated on the idea of this. Gradually the roof of the carriage began to assume a dome-like appearance and become semi-transparent. The hands of the unfortunate passengers began to sprout twigs and leaves and the legs of some of them to resemble stems. However, I woke up before the dream could develop further.

Yves Delage writes of a more sophisticated form of scene control:

> I dream that I am being pursued by people who have designs on my life. They may be criminals, savages, or, on a number of occasions, soldiers of an enemy power at war with France. I am on the point of being caught; sometimes I have already been caught, when a thought occurs to me. I think that there is an admirable way of evading the attention of the pursuers: it is to hide in a cavern that is completely inaccessible because its entry is under water, and it cannot be entered without diving into a lake. Neither lake nor cavern present in my dream has an external mental image. This is simply a thought that comes into my mind as I run along a road or the corridors of a house. Instantly by act of will, I change the scene and translate it into another setting where there are the necessary lake and cavern. Sometimes, even, if I have already been captured, I set back the course of events and go back to a time before I had been taken, in order to make the action develop in another way and to give it another outcome. To this end I set everything, pursuers and pursued, at a great distance. I give myself a start in order to arrive first and unob-

served at a convenient point of the lake. Once there I dive and enter the cavern.

My own attempts at scene control in a lucid dream are within the context of the first and last of these accounts. I either travel to a location I wish to be or at times, like in nightmares, I will a scene change and in a super-imposition manner like the fade-in, fade-out technique of modern cinematography the scene transforms into my desires.

But are visual images the only factor in lucid dreams and their manipulation the objective of achieving the state of lucidity? The answer to both of these queries is no. All sensory modalities: visual, auditory, olfactory, gustatory, and tactile have been reported in lucid dreams (cf. Green pp.70-78). Also the direction of dream images or scenes is not the goal of lucidity. It merely serves as a source of wish fulfillment along with the more important aspect of revealing the extent of conscious control and observation of ones own stored impressions and hallucinatory faculties—in a word, subconscious. And yet if the subconscious can be consciously and logically inspected and directed then is it really a "sub" conscious; and are there, for that matter, truly different levels of mental activity as conventional psychology avers!

This is the fundamental question: what does the existence of lucid dreams mean for the classical concepts of dreams and personality? It is here where the phenomenon of lucid dreams merits inclusion in the psychological sciences; for what it can mean in the broader scope of human psyche. It obliges us then to investigate the effects of lucidity and its perceptual and volitional features on classical and contemporary theories of dreams and later to discuss the larger ramifications on the broader spectrum of human personality. To do so requires both the unique contributions of lucidity as well as laboratory data on ordinary dream studies.

Discussion will center on fine dream theorists: three psychologists—Freud, Jung and Adler; and two, Wilse Webb and David Foulkes giving a physiological and evolutionary theory on dreams. These first three were selected for both the time and range that span their respective adherents and the latter two for their non-psychological orientation, which will prove useful in my own postulation.

Freud, of course, conceived dreams to be a psychic release function whose purpose is to symbolically distort repressed drives so that they find acceptable satisfaction. The dream material is composed of primary process thought and presented in the form of manifest content from which the true latent content must be interpreted. It goes without saying that lucid dreams tend to question this theory. If dreams are subconscious wish fulfillment, what of the analytical thought of pre-lucid and lucid dreams? What of the critical awareness of lucidity? What of the conscious direction of dream images? Can Freud call logical determination of the dream condition a primary process thought? Can he define dream image and scene control as unconsciously-designed manifest content? Would he call walking through walls a symbolic distortion of a repressed drive? Not that the fact of lucidity refutes Freud but it does raise some interesting questions.

There is some experimental data, though, that might serve to discredit his drive release proposal. In one study, Dement and Wolpert (1958) found that drive release or wish fulfillment was not the primary function of dreams. In an investigation of fifteen dream reports of subjects who had gone without fluids for 24 hours it was discovered that only five had any manifest element pertaining to fluids. Similarly Rechtschaffen (1964) revealed evidence which indicates that input to the central nervous system from the body environment, as for example, a parched throat or empty stomach does not seem to elicit overly drive-reducing dream content.

David Foulkes in *The Psychology of Sleep*, 1966, comments on these findings: "Such findings, of course, are consonant with the viewpoint developed in chapter three that wish fulfillment is not the primary goal of dream activity. The dreamer is apparently not particularly interested in hallucinating a wish fulfillment of, for example, a glass of water, which will provide no genuine answer to his problem. These findings are also consistent with observation of the effects of systematic semi-starvation upon dream reports recalled without the aid of EEG/EOG detection: there was no increase in food or eating dreams."

Other evidence against Freud comes from pre-REM cognitive studies such as that done by Foulkes (1964). It was shown that in the sleep stages prior to dreaming wherein actual dream formation is believed to take place the mental processes are similar to relaxed waking cognition, and we find an absence of a "seething, libidinous turmoil, sharply at variance with waking thought", as Freud suggests. Surely a cleverly disguised distortion of powerful drives seems an improbable result of such processes.

In fact, there might be indications that the dream activity serves not for wish fulfillment of repressed emotions but instead for actual repression of ongoing wishful thought arising in a dream—the reverse, in other words, of Freud's contention. Jerome L. Singer (1966) discovered in experiments with waking fantasy that eye movements began when the repression of ongoing wishful thought was initiated. Whether or not this function is analogous in dreams to REM fantasy is open to polemics, but the idea is worthy of consideration.

Freud, then, finds no small amount of dissonance with both lucid dreams and experimental observations.

Carl Jung defined a dream as, "a fragment of involuntary psychic activity just conscious enough to be reproducible in the waking state." In contrast to Freud, he saw dreams not as a distorted drive satisfaction process but rather as a compensatory mental action composed of both personal and archetypal images. Compensation consists of "balancing and comparing different data or points of view so as to produce an adjustment or rectification." Archetypal images are those universal inherited symbols that are indigenous to the nature of man or culture (collective unconscious).

It is axiomatic that Jung's definition of dreams would not permit of lucid potentialities. Hardly dream lucidity and manipulation would be classified as "involuntary" or "just conscious." And yet Jung does not encounter the evidential ripostes that are leveled against Freud. Suppose we concede that some compensatory activity does proceed in dreams; the question of whether this function is merely one pattern of normal mental action during dreams or if it is the functionary nature and *causa finalis* of them still remains unanswered. At this point it seems reasonable to say that his hypothesis as is leaves too many "lucid" ends and does not account for all observable phenomena occurring during REM periods. As will be seen later, I utilize aspects of Jung's theory in my own hypothesis, most notably his conception of archetypal images.

The formulations most complementary with the condition of lucidity in dreams are those of Alfred Adler, who viewed dreams to be a mechanism designed as a forward looking form of mental thought whose goal is the solution of problems arising in the external social world. According to Foulkes, "In general Adler sees dreams as essentially continuous with waking forms of mental activity. Moreover, Adler views symbols as being used in sleeping thought much as in waking thought: as a means of expressing thought and feelings, not disguising them." This conception is relatively compatible with lucid dreams as lucid processes are composed of waking forms of mental activity such as interpretive and analytical thought.

However, the contention that the fundamental purpose of a dream is the solution of social problems finds variance in studies done on pre-REM cognition. As Foulkes suggests on the same study introduced earlier, "If we find little evidence of libido or hostility in the pre-REM thought from which dreams may be presumed to develop, neither do we find much evidence for the Adlerian assertion that representation of pressing personal problems of a more general character are active at and responsible for dream formation. Awakenings made at various points leading into REM-period onset and during the early seconds and minutes of REM periods do not corroborate, at least in any obvious manner, the position that dreams begin with affective or ideational "sore spots".

It would seem, therefore, that neither Freud, Jung nor Adler provide adequate explanations for dream activity, both lucid and ordinary. While each of their propositions might account for specific observations of dream content they fail to offer a compendious outline that would satisfy the question of why we dream.

Perhaps this failure lies in the psychological premise for their assumptions. By granting the psychological basis for dream existence their predications can only be as accurate as that basis. Yet the presence of dreams as an affective service device has not been established as studies on REM deprivation illustrate.

Originally the psychological basis for dreams was thought to be given verification when it was discovered that experimental subjects show a "need" for dream sleep when deprived of it. By preventing REM sleep in individuals it was found they tend to "make-up" for lost dream time on deprived nights by more frequent, intense, and longer REM periods on recovery nights (Fisher and Dement, 1963; Rivik and Foulkes, 1966). Also, prolonged dream deprivation produced behavioral disorders in both humans and animals (Dement, 1969).

These favorable conclusions were short lived, however, as subsequent investigation threw the affective service theory into doubt; for if dreams function for personality convalescence it would be expected that greater emotional conflict would require more extended dream repair. And yet this was found not to be the case. Monroe and Dement in separate studies revealed that there is no increase in REM frequency or duration in emotionally disturbed individuals and in some cases a decrease. I. Feinberg (1964) found that schizophrenics had less REM's; and P. Onheiber (1965) discovered that the REM sleep time of child schizophrenics does not differ from normal children.

Dement1s findings of behavioral disorders resulting from dream deprivation as proof of a psychological requirement, received a further set back with extended experimentation of prolonged REM deprivation. Halis, Hoedemaker, Jacobson and Lichtenstein (1964) found no substantiation to psychic change due to deprivation, while others (Webb and Agnew, 1965) found similar behavioral changes with stage 4 NREM sleep deprivation; and still others (Jouvet, 1965) discovered behavioral REM deprivation phenomena in cats. Here Foulkes' words are appropriate: "It seems unlikely that cats show these symptoms because they use their dreams as mechanisms for discharging tension or repressed impulses that accumulated during the day." Disregarding Foulkes' burlesque it is indicative of a widespread attitude that the primary reason for dreaming lies somewhere other than psychic release, conflict resolution, or compensation.

While dreams have been suggested to be nothing more than, as Nathaniel Kleitman has said, "an acquired habit", they do normally incur greater significance even in the obscure sects of physiological dream theorists. One such, Willis B. Webb of the University of Florida, considers dreams to be a source of internal stimulation resulting from the evolutionary compression of the sleep cycle from poly-phasic to diurnal patterns. This conception has received considerable support in research such as that by Roffwarg, Musio and Dement (1966) where studies of sensory pathways of dream impulse, pontine mechanisms in neonates, and cortical and sub-cortical structural characteristics indicate a positive relationship between REM sleep and sensory stimulation and maturation of higher brain centers.

My own criticism of Webb intersects two facets of his theory. First, if this stimulation is a result of evolutionary compression, what explains the presence of REM's in the sleep patterns of poly-phasic lower animals whose patterns have not been compressed into two extended periods? And second, if dreams are a source of pontine stimulation of higher cortical centers and under the direction of the primitive brain stem areas, what satisfies the unique cortical conscious and control elements of lucidity?

David Foulkes maintains that dreams serve as evolutionary protectors of sleep. He points out that in ascending stage 2 sleep the tendency is toward wakefulness and in more primitive societies where external surveillance was of great importance sleep usually ended here; but as the need for protection diminished dreams began functioning to direct mental attention away from external impulses and toward internal imagery, thereby preserving sleep. While this hypothesis finds agreement in specific psychological and physiological characteristics resulting from EEG and dream content reports along with thought activity reports of ascending stage 2 as recorded by Foulkes (1960); it fails to answer for REM's in non-domesticated animals where the need to monitor the environment has not diminished, nor does it explain how the "realistic" thought processes of stage 2 can continue into dreams via lucidity without awakening.

It remains after the presentation of both psychological and biological explanations of dreams that their precise purpose in the sleep process and personality of man is still unaccounted for in any definitive manner. What are dreams? Or for that matter, what is sleep? How do lucid dreams fit into the total process? These questions are, of course, ones of cosmic importance, their answers, at best speculative. And yet speculation is the precursor of natural law. Ideas formed a priori serve as experimental blueprints for discovery and inspection.

With this prefatory note I offer my own theory—admittedly conjecture but conjecture built on observable phenomena and logical determination. It will, naturally, not arrive at the truth of dreams but will strive toward that end to the extent of the material available and my capacities of formulation. Apropos of this, Mr. Ronald Clark, in his biography of Albert Einstein, remarks, "science might really be a search not for absolute truth, but for a succession of theories that would progressively approach the truth." If that is the case, then theory, if it is credible, might offer a link in this theoretical concatenation, a clue in this search.

I am required, however, to deal not with dreams alone since they do not exist as a disassociate entity but rather as part of a total life system; Ergo I will consider dreams, sleep, and wakefulness in a complete context and deal with the special aspects of dreams and lucid dreams after this relationship has been established.

Herewith a scenario of my hypothesis: I propose that dreams serve both a physiological and psychological function:

1. Biologically they are part of a continuing sleep-dream—wakefulness cycle designed for the conservation and exchange of mass and energy in the brain and nervous system.

    a. The waking state is a condition whereby the energy of (impulses from sensory stimuli (measured in ergs) is converted to neuron and cortical mass (protein) by the process of ("coded") RNA production. Memory of such impulses possibly is retained by the particular arrangement of protein formation and its subsequent prescribed synaptic action.

    b. The sleeping state designated by EEG stage 4 specifically is a process through which protein synthesis is halted (and possibly reversed) due to the disassociation of the RNA molecules. This breakdown releases free phosphate groups that utilize the discharged RNA energy to combine with ADP to form ATP, a necessary catalyst for cellular energy transfer and neuron metabolism.

    c. The dream state designated by EEG stage 1 REM is an internal stimulation activity composed of both genetic and acquired experiential energy. It serves to transfer the (DNA-)RNA-protein held energy into neuron and cortical mass via endogenous sensory impulse stimulation and further RNA production. This dream-produced RNA in turn serves as a source of energy and phosphate for ATP synthesis.

2. Psychologically, dreams are primal learning experiences resulting from both memory storage of and cortical response to dream stimuli; and composed of inherited and personal image and sequence; thus contributing to personality determination. *In utero* and in infants this function provides a precognitive organizational apparatus for later learning experiences. In adults this works for both reinforcement of acquired learning and presentation of innovative situations of personality and imaginative design.

3. The physiological basis for lucid dreams and analytical thought in sleep and dreams rests in the unique relationship of the higher centers of the brain with the controlling mechanisms of the pons and reticular formation. A feedback signaling system with these areas and the image regulatory areas of the hippocampus enable interpretation and discrimination of both internal dream stimuli and external sensory impressions. With this basis a dreamer can spontaneously or by experimental pedagogic means become aware of and possibly control the dream experience thereby enabling the regulation of the personality determinants involved and the dream learning situation. Such lucidity, then, can release enormous therapeutic potential for self discovery and anxiety attenuation.

NOTES ON PART III

1. The ubiquitous Don Juan of Carlos Castaneda's *Journey to Ixtlan* suggests that to maintain the dream environment one should look at one's hands in the dream, as the other images tend to become evanescent once awareness has become established. However by focusing attention on the hands of the perceptual body the consciousness stabilizes the scene enough to move on to other images.

This has not been necessary in ray own experience nor in the others I have read where either mere desire or concentration upon surrounding images was sufficient to sustain the hallucinatory condition. Here again it appears that the method itself is not as important as faith in the particular method. As in flying, the result seems to be no more than an imaginative creation of a believed outcome of a given technique.

2. Sensory experimentation can be one of the most fascinating activities in lucid dreams. Van Eeden writes of finding a glass of wine in a dream, tasting it and exclaiming that it had the flavor of any of the best wines he had tasted in waking life. In one of my lucid states I was flying high above the town where I was living and I was feeling so free and wonderful that I wished I could hear at that moment Judy Garland singing "Somewhere over the Rainbow"; and no sooner had I thought it than in glorious multi-phonic sound the song filled the sky and sent me doing aerial acrobatics to the music. I Think of the possibilities: sampling exotic foods concocted by the imagination; listening to a symphony composed by the inner sources of creativity and conducted by one's self in a dream coliseum; discovering fields of iridescent flowers six feet high. As Dorothy said in Munchkin-land: "I don't think we're in Kansas anymore."

PART IV: SLEEP-DREAM-WAKEFULLNESS CYCLE AS SYSTEM FOR CONSERVATION AND EXCHANGE OF MASS AND ENERGY

As all fathers seem to incur a degree of believability that others lack, so too does Hans Berger, father of modern EEG sleep and dream research and inventor of the electroencephalograph, accede to a position of authority when he predicated the processes of mental activity to be subject to the laws of conservation of energy and dependant on physiochemical mechanisms which fully obey the laws of conservation of energy and thermodynamics. It is within this frame of reference that I turn the subject of sleep and dreams. However, I must add a further notion: that of Dr. Einstein's emendation to those laws to include the relationship of mass and its conservation.

As already presented, my apprehension of the sleep-dream-wakefulness cycle (SDW) is that it is one designed for the conservation and exchange of mass and energy in the brain and nervous systems. The primary components of this system are sensory energy measured in ergs (say, for example, photoelectric energy); nerve impulse energy; RNA production, energy and arrangement; protein formation; and ADP-ATP reaction energy. In order to show the SDW cycle as a process of energy and mass exchange it will be necessary to display a positive relationship between these components. But first I have a little story as a way of introduction.

Once there was a human brain and nervous system that after six months of its conception had almost all the ten billion neurons it would ever have. In order for the brain to develop, then, it could only increase in neuron size by protein formation. And for this protein to synthesize, a certain amount of energy needed to be supplied by the cell using a substance known as ATP (adenosine tri-phosphate) as a catalyst for energy transfer in cytoplasm. And yet, unfortunately for the neurons, they had little reserve of glycogen to account for the high metabolism energy needs of the cells and rate of ATP-ADP reactions. Thus, this energy for ATP production and protein synthesis needed to be provided by other means than food sources.

To the rescue came a molecule known as RNA (ribonucleic acid) which not only being the blueprint for protein formation, had the unique capability of being able to be produced from sensory and motor impulse energy. And, luckily for ATP, when one of the bases of this molecule disassociated, it released just enough energy to add a phosphate to ADP and form ATP for cell metabolism. However, as long as the rate of RNA synthesis exceeded that of its decomposition ATP production would not proceed. Therefore, a way needed to be found to stop or at least reduce sensory (and motor) impulses and RNA formation. Plants and simpler animals do not have to worry about this problem as they receive energy for ATP manufacture directly from photoelectric sources or food oxidation. But the evolutionary panacea solved it anyway for the higher orders: by creating sleep, a process where sensory impulses are to a degree excluded and the ratio of RNA synthesis/RNA disassociation enables the energy and phosphate release necessary for ATP production and subsequent protein development.

And yet there was another problem to be solved; for in the embryo where there is no sensory environment to speak of there could not be sufficient afferent impulse-produced RNA available for ATP formation and protein synthesis. This was solved, however, by the use of dreams; a DNA-RNA energy transfer system whereby RNA synthesis takes place through endogenous sensory impulse in the form of inherited images.

Still a third question remains: If the evolutionary apparatus has been so resourceful in solving the metabolism problems of the neurons why did it short change them of food energy (glycogen) in the first place? Good question—possible answer: perhaps this mechanism is somewhat of an energy fail safe device, for if the body must rely on the brain and nerves for function and if the brain is forced to rely only on bodily supplied food energy for metabolism then "who came first, the chicken or the egg?" And what is to prevent a vicious circle of atrophy: the lowering of brain metabolism due to a reduction in food energy and in turn an attrition of bodily activity due to reduced neuron metabolism. However, recent experimentation reveals that some safeguard system is indeed at work; for in studies with adult rats that have been starved to death, the body weight is reduced to half but the brain of the animal loses no weight whatsoever! (Halacy, *Man and Memory*, 1970) This result is indicative of a brain metabolism independent of food sources and supportive of an energy fail—safe mechanism—perhaps the RNA-ATP relationship discussed.

It has been proposed (Ansel and Richter, 1954) that the decomposition of protein and utilization of amino acids might provide for the missing energy. Yet this would give no answer for why the brain loses no weight during starvation, for surely the cannibalism of its own cellular protein for energy would involve a loss in brain mass. Also this would be a pretty worthless safety valve system since in the absence of glycogen the effect would by similar to a pendulum: protein synthesis never quite approaching protein breakdown due to the energy lost in metabolism.

Such confabulation aside, I shall proceed to the systematic investigation of each facet of my SDW theory.

As far as the brain and nervous system are concerned, the condition of wakefulness is one that provides for the formation of brain protein for impulse and memory functions. This protein needs three fundamental requirements for synthesis: amino acids, energy via ATP-ADP reaction and RNA for design. All of course are present in the neuron in its initial development. Although, as suggested before, the glycogen available for energy is inadequate for extended protein development. Thus, energy for ATP formation must be obtained from the breakdown of RNA in the cells. But if ATP uses RNA breakdown for energy, then protein would have to do without it for synthesis design. So some way must be provided that insures RNA for both protein formation and decomposition for ATP manufacture and metabolism. It was: they took turns.

The provision of RNA for protein formation is supplied by the waking state where sensory stimulation contributes energy for RNA and protein manufacture. Extensive research has been done in this area. Hamberger and Hyden (1949) and Brattgard (1952) obtained evidence of an initial increase in RNA due to brief or mild stimulation of nerve cells. Chentsov, Baroviagin and Brodskii (1961) reported rapid changes in RNA content of retinal ganglion cells when stimulated by light. Brattgard (1952) also found that the retinal ganglion of rabbits reared in darkness lacked the normal complement of RNA and protein. Hyden and Pigon (1960) discovered a 4.5% increase in RNA and 14% increase in protein weight after stimulation of the vestibular nerves in rabbits. G.P. Falwar in Delhi showed that exposure to light of an animal reared in darkness resulted in an increase of RNA and protein synthesis in its visual cortex. In 1968 B. Machlus and J. Gaitu of New York University revealed evidence of synthesis of RNA in mice involved in learning. In long-time experiments in which rats were reared in different environments Bennet (1964) found that constant exposure to sensory stimulation increased overall weight and protein content of the cerebral cortex in comparison; also the weight of specific sensory receptive areas of the brain could be increased with respective sensory stimulation. Hyden and Egyhazi (1962, 1963, 1964) learned that in two groups of rats, one receiving sensory stimulation from rotating, the other from learning situations; both had increased RNA content (6-10%) in nerve cells of specific receptive areas (also the messenger RNA in the learning rats changed its base ratio of adenine/guanine to favor adenine considerably). While not all experiments have been reflective of these findings there does seem to be some causal relationship between sensory impulse and RNA formation.

In my own efforts to quantify this relationship I encountered a surprising energy similitude: (while this similitude is only concerned with the relation of photoelectric energy it might prove suggestive of a more general equation). The energy of one quantum of light of a frequency within the visible spectrum can be calculated using Mr. Planck's constant to average in the vicinity of 10(13) ergs. A nerve pulse of about 120 mill volts imparts an energy quantity of 10(13) ergs. (Halacy, p.196) The amount of energy required to synthesize one base of an RNA molecule is approximately 10(13) ergs (Fohg 1969). If there appears to be numerical tautology here, that is correct. At the very least, if this is coincidence, then nature's discretion leaves much to be desired.

I leave my primary illustration of this theoretical function of wakefulness at this point. Still it must be observed as it is widely debated elsewhere that RNA might be a memory engram that is "coded" for protein arrangement and future prescribed synaptic action. Studies in support of RNA as the essential memory unit determined by the make-up of its bases include the following: Dingman and Sporn (1961) injected rats with RNA inhibitor drugs and found that "memory traces in the nervous system are produced by the formation of altered RNA." Similarly Flexner and Stellar (1967) used puromycin to block RNA and found that memory in mice was impaired or cancelled. This prompted Flexner to write in *Science*, 1967, "We assume that the initial learning experience triggers synthesis of one or more species of messenger RNA. This m RNA alters the synthetic rate of one or more proteins which are essential for the expression of memory." In another experiment Frank Morrell of Stanford found in duplicated memory brain lesions that the mirror memory focus lesions contained higher RNA than nearby normal tissue. Dr. D. Ewin Cameron, McGill University reported that elderly patients receiving doses of yeast RNA had improved memories and that the RNase (a RNA prohibitory) level was higher in poor memory cases. E. Roy John at the University of Rochester discovered that planarians placed in an enzyme that breaks down RNA were prohibited from regenerating learning as had been found earlier in normal worms. Allen Jacobson of University of California found that RNA extracted from trained rats produced learned responses in untrained recipients.

And yet conversely, Barondes and Jarvik (1961), using actinomycin—D (messenger RNA inhibitor) learned that although the synthesis of RNA in the mouse brain was inhibited by 83% for several hours the animals were able to learn and remember as well as controls in a simple passive avoidance conditioning situation.

The exact rate of RNA and protein in the memory process is still in doubt; but both the biochemical nature of nerve metabolism and the evidence presented here merit at least inspection in this sense and possible later use in terms of this paper in conceptual constructions of a larger scope. RNA synthesis, however, for purposes here, was considered more in the context of its position in an energy-mass relationship than a memory process. Hopefully it was this feature that has been demonstrated.

Once the waking state has had its turn to produce RNA for brain mass design from sensory impulse it is in order for sleep to reverse this process for purposes of ATP energy supply and cortical mass control. It must be emphasized that when referring to sleep it is specifically intended to mean EEG stage 4, as I will defer to Mr. Webb's (*Sleep: An experimental Approach*, 1968) description of EEG stage 2 and 3 as stages designed for competition between the need for deep sleep and the need to monitor the environment as evidenced by studies on instrumental behavior during sleep (Williams, Morlock, Morlock, 1966).

I consider sleep, then, to be a process where external sensory impulse is reduced or rather not reinforced by such areas as the reticular formation (Moruzzi and Mazoun, 1949) and internal sensory image formation prohibited by a desynchronization of the hippocampus (Douglas 1967); and thereby considerably lowering RNA and protein formation. This reduction of RNA synthesis enables the rate of disassociation due to RNase to exceed formation and thus release expendable energy and free phosphate molecules for addition to ADP to form ATP for energy transfer (also in some instances released adenine might provide for manufacture of ATP from raw materials).

For corroboration I refer to causal and molecular observations. The first of these is the discovery (Luby, et. al., 1960) that after about four days of sleep deprivation production of the catalyst ATP in the nervous system almost ceases. Now since blood supply to the brain has not diminished during these extended periods of wakefulness, the lack of ATP cannot be explained by any deprivation of bodily supplied energy. Some other normal energy source must have been cut off. I suggest that this source was the breakdown of RNA; and since the continuous influx of sensory impulse sustained a high synthetic equilibrium there was no expendable energy (or possibly phosphate) for ATP formation.

Other experimental observations yield the following results: constant exposure to light increased NREM sleep time in rats (Fishman and Roffwarg, 1972); human subjects submerged in water for 24 hours required only two hours of sleep (Graveline, et. al., 1961). These results, perhaps, are supportive of the argument that NREM sleep duration and RNA breakdown/ATP formation are directly proportionate to the amount of sensory stimulation received when awake. Greater stimulation would mean increased RNA and protein synthesis which in turn would require more ATP for the increased metabolic activity; ATP in turn having larger sensory-produced RNA reserves from which to draw upon.

Also, upon molecular simulation the RNA molecule reveals an arrangement of nitrogenous bases (adenine, guanine, etc.) interpolated by phosphate units with a phosphate on each end. Disassociation would release first a free phosphate and one of the bases. The energy emitted by the "break away" of one of these bases would be the same as its synthesis: 10(13) ergs—which just happens to be about the same amount required to add a phosphate to ADP to form ATP in photosynthesis (R.P. Levine, *Readings from Scientific American*, December 1969; and quantum mechanics). Fancy that!

While this somewhat disjunctive data proves nothing by itself, it does intimate; and such intimations together with the presence of unexplainable phenomena like the high metabolism of neurons without an adequate internal supply of energy can yield hypothesis for later investigation.

Another regulatory function of sleep might be neuron and brain size control; for if nerve cells grow in volume and weight with use, sensory impulse, and learning, then what is to prevent their unchecked growth; and what is to stop the brain from theoretically growing too large for the skeletal enclosure? Admittedly this is a little far fetched, but conceivably within the range of factual extrapolation.

My proposal is that by the reduction of RNA formation and the breakdown of these protein structural molds, protein synthesis itself is halted and possibly reversed during sleep! It has been shown that the neuron contains a proteinase capable of breaking down protein (Ansell and Richter, 1954). Also if the disassociation of protein at synapses is involved in electrochemical impulse formation as has been suggested (Hyden, 1959, 1962) then this large amount of protein decomposition during sleep might account for the high amplitude of EEG. stage 4 delta waves. In fact, Edward Evarts reported in *Progress in Brain Research* v.18, 1965, that slow wave impulse in sleep can be traced to the larger neurons—perhaps protein rich neurons in a state of de-synthesis.

Naturally, I am aware that little has been established in the way of a prima fascia case for my theory on sleep function, yet there have been some interesting interrelationships explored.

With that, I move on to the locus of dreams in this SLW cycle. As told in my little prefatory tale, dreams as designated by EEG stage 1 REM originally evolved to provide a endogenous source of sensory energy stimulation for RNA and protein synthesis and later ATP formation. Roffwarg, Muzio and Dement (1966) established a possible relationship between REM's and brain development in neonates that might provide an experimental basis for my own speculative extensions. They summarize their findings as such:

> The REM mechanism serves as an endogenous source of stimulation, furnishing great quantities of functional excitation to higher centers. Such stimulation would be particularly crucial during periods *in utero* and shortly after birth, before appreciable stimulation is available to the central nervous system. It might assist in structural maturation and differentiation of key sensory and motor areas with the central nervous system, partially preparing them to handle the enormous rush of stimulation provided by the postnatal milieu, as well as contributing to their further growth after birth. The sharp diminution of REM sleep with development may signify that the mature brain has less need for endogenous stimulation.

This view would not be inconsistent with my own that REM's function in fetus and infant to provide genetic (DNA) energy for RNA-protein-ATP reactions. Without such stimulation and energy there is evidence that structural maturation and maintenance are seriously impaired (Hyden, 1943)(Nissen, Chow, Semmes, 1951)(Rosenweig, Bennet, Krech, 1964). Yet the exact relationship of REM and RNA-protein has found little conclusion. Investigation conducted by Jouvet, Zimmerman and others reveal a possible correlation between the dream state and cortical RNA-protein synthesis; but this is far from definitive.

My own hypothesis of the nature of REM's for brain growth and energy for ATP results not from any singular group of findings but from the inclusion of such hypothesis in the total SDW cycle and the resulting logical formulations. If RNA and protein production has been shown to be an obbligato of sensory energy exchange in the waking state, it is reasonable to conclude that since DNA is capable of releasing RNA for subsequent neural protein and this protein in turn is a contributory to impulse formation, then these impulses emitting from the pons in the fetus develop the higher brain areas in the same manner as waking impulses. This RNA and protein development from dreams is reversed during NREM sleep in the manner suggested before and used for ATP energy functions and mass regulation.

Dreams, then, in the fetus and infant serve to develop brain mass for later learning (as degree of learning capacity is dependent on cortical mass—Lashley, 1929) and to supply RNA for ATP energy. Looking at the NREM-REM cycle in neonates the EEG recordings reflect such a process at work. It can be seen that early in gestation the fetus spends practically 100% of sleep time in REM's (Parmelee, Akiyana, Wenner, Flescher, 1964), accounting for a high volume of stimulation for RNA-protein synthesis and neuron growth. At 35 weeks this percentage is reduced to 67%—explaining a rise of the need for ATP beyond glycogen provision due to the high synthetic metabolic rate sustained; this ATP being provided for during increased NREM sleep processes via RNA disassociation. By birth, the percentage of REM time is 50%, signifying a more developed brain for waking functions and greater sleep time for energy requirements of such functions.

If dreams perform a building and energy role in early stages of life, what biological purpose would they serve in adults where both brain maturation and sensory energy are well supplied without them? Sensory deprivation experiments might suggest an answer. When external sensory stimulation is deprived of waking subjects they begin shortly to form internal images (Bexton et al., 1954) or hallucinations (Ziskind and Ougsberg, 1962); and when specific areas of the brain and nervous system receive no sensory or motor energy required for that area the REM's of the subject show a predominance of that specific deprived stimulation (Whitman, Pierce, 1960), (Wood, 1962). Inductively then, dreams in adults might provide energy for protein and RNA functions in specific areas of the brain deprived of it during wakefulness and NREM sleep.

Enough of biochemistry.

Fundamental Question: are dreams learning experiences; and if so are they learning experiences before birth? Also, if they are, to what extent do they influence personality? A simple practical reference yields an immediate answer to the former: a boy dreams of crashing in a plane; henceforth he is afraid of the sound of jets—he learned. While this somewhat pedestrian example doesn't say much in itself, it does provide a universal observational foundation for logical development of the question.

Physiological data collected on subjects during the REM state offers considerable material on the relationship of dreams and learning by providing reports on the similarity of dream stimuli and response to the waking experience. Most ostensible are the EEG recordings of the dreaming condition and the occurrence of eye movements in association with it (Aserinsky and Kleitman, 1953). The EEG's of subjects in ascending stage 1 REM reveal an activated desynchronized pattern of alertness accompanied by physiological changes in the body such as increased cortical temperature and blood flow, faster heartbeat, irregular breathing, higher basal skin resistance; all of which are the normal signals of waking response to experience. In several studies (Dement and Wolpert, 1958, Roffwarg et. al., 1962, Greenberg, 1966) it was demonstrated that dream images are associated with ocular movements in pursuit of them, similar to wakeful action. (However, experiments by Jouvet et. al., 1951, indicate that REM's are neither confined to or evoked exclusively from dream image pursuits).

In this same context of learning or waking-like bodily and cortical response to dream stimuli, research has shown that the similarity of dreaming cortical response to waking is evidenced by the form and amplitude of the EEG response to stimuli in cats, rabbits, monkeys, chimps, adult and newborn humans. Also muscular and receptive areas of the body react similarly, if diminutively, during dreams to waking behavioral response to stimuli: McGuigon and Fannel (1971) found significant covert oral behavior during REM's where there were conversational dreams. Baust, Berlucchi and Moruzzi (1964) discovered that "even the modulations of tone in the fine muscles of the middle ear show phasic and tonic changes during REM's just as they do in animals responding actively to waking events." Wolpert (1960) reported that in REM sleep upper motor neuron activity is markedly increased, spikes in the extra-ocular muscles are coordinated with discharge in the visual afferent system, and phasic bursts of muscle potentials may accompany hallucinated movement. In one case he observed "action potential in wrist muscles during REM periods tended to be associated with dream reports including the hallucination of wrist involved activity such as picking up something with the hands."

These results show a positive association between dream stimuli and neural muscular response in a manner analogous to waking behavior. The subjects in these cases are reacting to the dream situation as if it were a waking experience (although on a less intense level). If we examine the impulse pathway taken by a dream image a possible reason for this "real" response to internal stimuli can be seen. Webb comments, "already there is evidence that the normal neuron-ana-tomical routes to the cortex are traveled by REM state impulses in the visual sen-sory system after they arrive at the lateral genticulate body from the pons." Dement suggests that, "once this internal sensory input is substituted in the stim-ulus-response chain, higher centers interpret and react to it as if it were a set of true percepts impinging on the central nervous system from without."

If the response to dream stimuli is physiologically analogous to normal waking response, then it is reasonable to conclude that dreams are fundamental learning experiences. This conclusion is founded on two premises. First a learning situa-tion entails a reaction to an accepted set of sensory impressions and as has been demonstrated the cortex accepts the dream impressions as real and reacts accord-ingly. Second, memory of such impression and response must be consolidated for learning to take place; and given the theoretical relationships of dreams and RNA and RNA/protein and memory it might be assumed that the necessary memory requirements for learning are present-at least in a low energy or "subconscious" fashion. Furthermore, if dreams are learning events then it is axiomatic that they will influence personality and behavior at least to a subliminal extent. It advances beyond my capacities to discuss exactly where dreams place themselves in person-ality determination, but a sophisticated form of content analysis demonstrating the relationship between dreams and waking behavior can be found in a recent publication (Lind and Hall, 1970).

But what of infants and fetal personages in this regard? Do they learn from REM dreams or, in fact, do they dream at all in the normal sense of the word? And if they do, what do they dream of since their personal experience is infinites-imal?

There is no conclusive evidence to demonstrate that infants and fetuses actu-ally dream images or events but there are some provocative findings that confirm some sort of visual activity taking place *in utero*. It was reported (E.V. Evarts, 1962, Jouvet et. al. 1964) that phasic activity in the genticulate body and occipi-tal cortex is synchronous with REM bursts in fetus. O.R. Langworthy found in 1933 that there is substantial myelinization in the visual system before birth; and J.L. Cone, 1939, discovered that the sensory neurons of the striate cortex were second in development only to the Betz cells of the pyramidal tract. All these results indicate a system of internal visual activity before birth.

That this activity is in the form of perceptual images, however crude, is a moot conception. Some experimentation, though, reinforces such a notion: In as inves-tigation conducted by Robert L. Fantz (1961) who tested 30 infants aged one to

15 weeks at weekly intervals with different test patterns it was revealed that the differential response to the patterns by all ages tested indicated that form perception is not a result of post natal acquired learning but is somehow already present at birth. In another experiment Fantz tested 49 infants from 4 days to 6 months old with three patterns: one with a stylized face in black on a pink background, another with scrambled facial features, and a third with a solid patch of black equal in size to the facial area of the others. The results were the same for all ages—the infants look mostly at the real face, less often at the scrambled pattern and ignored the solid control pattern. Interpreting these results Fantz states, "The experiment suggests that there is an unlearned, primitive meaning in the form perception of infants..." Could this primitive meaning be nothing more than memory of dream images of human faces presented in REM periods?

Going back to my SDW cycle, if REM's do provide a source for protein formation and if as presented earlier protein synthesis is a result of learning (Samuel Barondes, NY. University), then a possible syllogistic equation might exist between REM's in fetuses and infants and learning.

If we suppose that there possibly is image perception, though crude, and learning processes in neonates then where would these images come from and what would the dream learning event consist of? Carl Jung with his exegetical "archetypal image" hypothesis provides an answer: dreams in early pre and post natal humans consist of inherited images of a collective unconscious which are indigenous to a culture, society or nature of man. They are nondescript epiphenomena symbolic of the universal and cultural forces in man.

I would propose something a little more specific. I consider dreams in neonates to be composed of genetic transferred experience and images conveyed through DNA-produced RNA and protein. Depending on the specific character of the DNA inherited memory images might be of ones parents, great grandparents or ancestry ad infinitum. This conception would not be inconsistent with either the theory of internal pons stimulation presented by Dement or the DNA-RNA-memory propositions formulated by Hyden, 1964.

The psychological function of this in neonates might be some sort of primal learning device that provides a precognitive organizational apparatus for later learning experiences in life. Jung opines that these archetypal dreams could be the instinctual device long sought for: "the instincts (inborn, unlearned tendencies) form very close analogies to the archetypes—so close, in fact, that there is good reason for supposing that the archetypes are the unconscious images of the instincts themselves; in other words, they are patterns of instinctual behavior." Okay, I'll go along with that but only to the extent that such patterns of instinctual behavior are only one of many patterns available in fetal and infant dreams, as the memory traces present through DNA would not be confined to mere instinctual experience.

In adults, a psychological function of dreams aside from any psychic service for personality might be a method of learning and memory reinforcement by replication of internal memory impulse accumulated during waking. In experiments with mice scientists found that by depriving them of REM sleep the mice forgot electroshock training that had been administered before sleeping. Also, at a 1969 meeting of the Association for the Psycho-Physiological Study of Sleep, it was reported that chicks who learn in the first day of life most of what they will ever know, spend nearly all the time they are asleep during the first 24 hours in REM sleep. In a related vein, research into ablation or disease of the hippocampus which plays a image regulatory role in sleep and dreams (Horowitz, 1963) finds that such ablation causes memory defects (Rose and Symonds, 1960, Richter, p.158). From these results it may be supposed that dreams exhibit a short-term to long-term memory characteristic that scientists have sought. Along these lines, Derek Richter (1966) reflects, "Clinical observations suggest that active repetitive processes may be involved in memorizing and also in the strengthening of certain memories with the passage of time." Biologically, perhaps these repetitive processes are protein impulse recycling through dreams into identically coded RNA and further protein for memory reinforcement. Psychologically this would mean that learned experience behavior is both strengthened in dreams and modified by the juxtaposition of acquired and inherited memory traces.

Assuming that dreams do possess a capacity for innovative, genetic, and replicated learning experience in both adults and neonates and such experience influences personality, then at initial inspection this contention would appear to decimate contemporary efforts at personality analysis: for if dreams cause behavior rather than merely symbolically reflect it, where does one begin to look for causal agents of psyche formation since those agents might entail any number of past and inherited memories and imaginative or sub-conscious arrangement of them. And yet these revelations are not as cataclysmic as might seem at first. For it has been obvious for some time that a character and personality are determined by both ones own personal experiences and hereditary propensities and it is doubtful that although dream images and events might reorganize into new situations for stimulus-response learning, the material available and the manner of dream content development to be outlined later would limit the seemingly multitudinous behavioral learning possibilities and present the individual with personality determinants not altogether unexpected given the persons past events and hereditary traits.

NOTES ON PART IV

1. In normal cellular circumstance the lack of glycogen resources would not in itself be such a problem, as glucose could by-pass the glycogen stage of metabolism and be reduced directly from glucose to glucose 1-phosphate and glucose 2-phosphate and then to pyruvic acid for oxidation. However, in the nerve cell there is a high propensity for glucose to be processed into glutamate for amino acid formation and further protein synthesis (to wit, Ansell and Rickter, 1964, injected Cl-glucose into the nerve cell and found that 70% of it was used for amino acid production as compared to 2% in the blood cells and 9% in the liver cells—leaving the nerve with little free glucose for energy purposes). Thus glycogen, safe from protein seduction, becomes of primary importance to the energy needs of the cell.

The important thing here is not so much the RNA molecule count, as that count has been shown in some cases to remain constant or even decrease under stimulation, but rather the RNA base count as individual bases can be added to existing molecules or combine two or more molecules, thus accounting for no change or reduction in the total number of separate molecules. Richter, Aspects of Learning and Memory, cites cases where an increase of a specific base composition was discovered without any change in the RSN molecule count)

2. It must be remembered that while the actual transfers that serve to store energy in the RNA. are between the nerve impulse and the bases of RNA, the nerve impulse has itself been initiated by the absorption of various sensory stimuli, producing a triggering effect of depolarizing the membrane of the receptor cell which incites the permeability and flow of sodium and potassium ions and, in turn, causes an action potential that gives rise to an impulse. The process of depolarization, once triggered, has its own regenerative effect due to the change of electrical charge and ions between the cytoplasm and the membrane. Thus an impulse generated from a receptor cell expends no intrinsic energy (ATP); throughout either impulse formation or potential recovery; rather it appears to utilize electromagnetic, mechanical or chemical energy from the environment to effect the trigger of depolarization. The precise method by which external energy is utilized remains unknown-. In photo-excitation of the rod cells photon energy is absorbed for isomerization of rhodopsin and this somehow effects the trigger. But unfortunately little is known exactly how light, touch, smell, or sound ultimately engenders the depolarization of the membrane.

DeForest Mellon in The Physiology of Sense Organs, 1968, summarizes the sensory mechanism as follows: "The detection of environmental stimuli by sensory systems may be conveniently regarded as three sequentially arranged processes; (l) the absorption of stimulus energy; (2) the utilization of the absorbed energy to effect micro-structural changes in specific regions of the membrane of the sensory cell, and (3) the initiation of nerve impulses."

3. It may seem somewhat strange that sleep deprivation should cut off almost all ATP production, since although RNA supplied energy ceases due to a high sensory-synthetic rate the nervous system still would be receiving blood-supplied sources for ATP formation. Yet it must be remembered that during extended wakefulness the prodigious synthesis of protein would consume practically all available glucose and amino acids and once the supply of glycogen is used up the cell would run out of gas8 as it were. Another conjecturable possibility is that during deprivation all free phosphate molecules are used up in forming the increased quantities of RNA, and even if there were an available energy source from ATP, there would not be enough phosphate to back it up.

4. Recent experimentation further supports the theoretical relationship of sensory stimulation/protein synthesis and energy storage in RNA, and sleep disassociation for ATP. J. Tagney in *Brain Research* v.53, 1973, reported that rats raised in a sensory enriched environment had significantly more NREM sleep than the deprived rats and those that were changed from a deprived to an enriched setting had 15% increased NREM sleep time after sixteen days in the new environment. The conclusion of this is that increased sensory input and impulses create larger amounts of RNA storehouses and longer periods of NREM sleep are needed to break down the molecules for ATP formation.

5. The energy required for production of ATP from ADP in photosynthesis vas determined using the voltage differentials between various electron donors and receptors along a gradient in the cell. These differentials that provide energy for the addition of a phosphate to ADP are reflective of the energy received from a photon striking a molecule of H_2O and forcing an electron along the gradient. Therefore the energy required for ATP is the same as the energy transmitted by a quantum of light and can be found using the formula $E = H \times V$ where H is Planck's constant and V is the frequency. I simply took the average result of such an equation.

6. That REM sleep serves to provide stimulation to the nervous system and areas of the brain deprived of it during waking activity is further evidenced by such studies as those of Fishman, Ross, and Roffwag, *Experimental Neuroloy*, v.36, 1972, where it was found rats that were confined in continuous darkness had a 30% increase in REM sleep during the first two weeks. Likewise, continuous light reduced REM sleep. Now it may be argued that dreams are actually providing no net increase in energy (ATP) to the nervous system since it would require energy to initiate the dream Impulses and thus nothing is really gained overall. However, as REM's originate in the pontine region of the reticular formation and the reticular formation is also a focal point for afferent sensory Impulses it might be that the pons works as a sort of energy withholding unit that saves up impulse energy for rainy days and distributes it to the deprived areas via dreams.

7. A concept of inherited experience in dreams is at best an. audacious speculation and belongs to a family of theory that has long been considered untenable. How an event of ones progenitors, even if encoded in RKA in the nerve cells, could possibly be passed on to the offspring via DNA in reproductive cells is quite inconceivable at this time. Some would admit of certain general experience of a species that arises out of the species evolution to become an innate part of genetic action; but few would extend this to acquired experience within an immediate group of generations. However, recent discoveries in both physiology and psychology such as those of Author Janov, *The Feeling Child*, 1972, have revealed a heretofore-unknown interrelationship between memory and all bodily cells. These discoveries might support, then, a connection between the acquired experience, storage in reproductive cells, and eventual transfer from the pons through dreams back into cortical memory engrams. Of course, the precise mechanism by which this takes place remains unsolved. All I needed, though, was the existence of observable phenomena that could not be accounted for by psychological or physiological theories extant (e.g. the reappearance of an identical bruise incurred at birth and materializing again years later) and I'll say anything.

PART V:
PHYSIOLOGICAL BASIS FOR LUCID DREAMS AND NATURE OF DREAM AND LUCID DREAM THOUGHT

Returning to the ascendant purpose of this paper, it is necessary to ascertain what this preceding theory means for lucid dreams and also to attempt to provide a possible physiological basis for "lucidity". Along with this will be an effort to display the particular analytical and discriminative aspects of sleep and dreams that provide a background for spontaneous lucidity and experimentally induced lucid dreams.

If dreams originated as a source of stimulation for neuron development and energy provision and assumed a collateral learning feature, then what does all this hold for the phenomenon of lucid dreams? I feel that this means lucidity is vindicated by this theory as a natural and salutary function rather than a violation of established psychological processes. For if dreams act to build protein, provide energy and contribute to memory and learning then they are primarily a biological and behavioral influence rather that a psychological adjustment or integration mechanism. Thus they are not a requirement of a normal adaptive emotional state through psychic release, compensation or social planning. Indeed these devices might be at work in dreams but in the event of their absence no evidence has proven a detrimental effect on the personality of the individual. Hence, the fact of being aware in a dream of ones own position in time and space, knowing that the experience is of an imaginative illusionary nature, usurps no psychological authority and violates no ongoing emotional "out patient."

To demonstrate lucid dreams as a natural extension of normal dream thought requires first an inquiry into the encephalic sleep-dream apparatus and its possible implication for lucid theory.

The consensus seems to place the primary control mechanism for sleep within the midbrain reticular formation (Magoun and Morruzi, 1949, Bremmer, 1935) and is labeled the "ascending reticular activating system" (ARAS). It had long been thought that reduced sensory stimulation was the initiator of sleep as could be inferred from observation of a person going to bed at night (shuts off lights, turns off radio, etc.). However, Lindsley (1950) found that lesions in the sensory tract alone did not result in sleep wherein lesions of the reticular formation that left the sensory tracts intact did result in sleep. And Oswald (1960) reported that in experiments, subjects went into sleep while their eyes were taped open and they were receiving discomforting electrical shocks on the back of the knee joint while at the same time these shocks were synchronized with the rhythm of very loud jazz music and powerful lights were flashed on and off in front of the subjects face. Clearly then, while reduced or increased sensory stimulation can affect the sleep cycle, sleep onset itself is under the overt control of some area of the brain—specifically the reticular formation.

How this operates is of the concern of David Foulkes: "When incoming sensory impulses are supported by impulses passing through the ARAS, one is awake and aware of the environmental events causing the sensory impulses. When the ARAS does not support incoming sensory stimulation, a person is not aware of environmental events causing such impulses and is asleep." Placing this hypothesis within the frame of my own concepts of RNA-ATP equilibrium, I propose that in waking the ARAS replicates sensory stimuli to significantly raise the amount of impulses coming from a stimuli and consequently the number of RNA units synthesized with protein following suit. When asleep the ARAS does not replicate and possibly inhibits sensory impulse, thus reducing RNA production and enabling a higher ratio of RNA breakdown needed for ATP formation to proceed.

Concerning the REM system, Jouvet and Moumier (1962) discovered the possible controlling mechanism of REM periods to be the pons area of the reticular formation. With ablation of the pontine area no REM sleep occurs although the sleep-waking cycle is maintained. Dement (1966) suggests that it is from this pontine area that the ersatz sensory impulses emanate in early development for maturation of the higher brain centers. In the context of my postulations the pons would be the site of cortical mass development and RNA-ATP manufacture throughout the nervous system.

Another location that is fundamentally involved in the sleep-dream cycle is the hippocampus. Hernandez-Peon (1963) have theorized that this part of the limbic system is the focal center of sleep. They believe that this hippocampus area controls the sleep state through descending connections from the pre-optic region of the hypothalamus to the reticular arousal system and its pontine mechanisms.

Two other observations of hippocampus activity are interesting. First, it has been found that the EEG characteristics of this area are in exact opposite to the ongoing EEG characteristics of the cortex. When the cortex is showing synchronous waves associated with sleep, the hippocampus is showing desynchronized fast waves and vice versa. Another, is the relation of the hippocampus to image formation: Maclean (1966) and Horowitz (1968) reported definite links between the hippocampus and image formation. According to Horowitz, "In experiments where images were stimulated by electrodes the hippocampus accounted for the single greatest response to stimulation in producing Type A images of externally placed content with formed objects" (dreamlike).

The clue to the physiological basis for lucid dreams lies in the relation of the cortex with its interpretive and analytical capacities to these areas discussed (reticular formation, pons, and hippocampus) and possible cortical influence on the SDW cycle, dream thought, and dream content. Nathaniel Kleitman introduced such cortical influence into SDW theory when he proposed that the cycle in adults was one of "wakefulness of choice" or volitional control over the sleep controlling mechanisms and patterns. In connection with this, Wilse Webb points out "that when animals like the dog or cat are deprived of their cortex, their sleep (which is normally characterized by long periods of sleep and waking similar to humans) becomes poly-phasic with short bursts of sleep or waking. Furthermore, such short bursts of sleep and waking are characteristic of human infants and young dogs and cats before their cortex is fully developed."

Reviewing recent experimentation in this area of cortex-brain stems relationships Leonard Stevens in *Explorers of the Brain* (1971) asserts that "continued investigation indicates that the reticular activating system goes to work not only when triggered by afferent sensory signals, but also when signaled by the cortex itself. In other words the cortical activity of a thought may operate the alarm system. Thus the brain alerts itself for action. This was demonstrated experimentally by electrical stimulation of the brain applied to a certain point on a monkey's cortex, causing the animal to suddenly perk up as if to say, 'What was that?'"

G.E. Wolstenholme in *The Nature of Sleep* elaborates on this relationship: "Experimental results show that the cerebral cortex exerts a descending tonic influence on the brain stem reticular formation. Cortical inhibitory effects control the acceptance and intra-reticular transaction of sensory impulses reaching the RF through collaterals of main sensory pathways." Wolstenholme suggests some reticular-cortex—reticular loop in operation.

The ramifications of these findings for this paper are twofold. Biologically and also parenthetically as the concern at this point is with psychological lucidity and its physical roots, this tonic influence on the SDW cycle in the brain stem might be in effect a chemical or enzyme sensitive to RNA-ATP equilibrium and protein metabolism. More importantly, these results are reflective of a discriminative and interpretive action of the cortex in processing external and internal (for reason of impulse routes discussed) sensory material before transfer to the reticular formation and its pontine areas-lucidity being an end result of such interpretation.

By inspection of the cortical-hippocampus interaction, a basis is approached for dream sequence and image control in lucid dreams. In electrical stimulation of images (Pribrom and Mclean, 1953) it was learned that the cortex "fired" into the hippocampus to produce images. Also, stimulation of specific cortical sensory areas resulted in hippocampus image formation (Horowitz, 1968). Consequently, it can be reasoned that the higher discriminative and voluntary regions of the brain could direct and control image formation in dreams via hippo-pontine association, as in lucid hallucinatory manipulation.

These physiological obligations at rest the psychological presence of analytical and interpretive thought in sleep and non-lucid dreams is under consideration as a premise for lucid determination.

Independent from laboratory discovery of logical or interpretive thought during sleep and dreams but homologous to it is the large historical and personal reflections available. Accounts of decisions or discovery in dreams have pervaded literature and legend for centuries. Samuel Coleridge avers that he composed his "Kubla Kahn" in its entirety while sleeping. Otto Loewi made his Nobel-prize winning discovery of chemical nerve transmission in a dream. Friedrick von Kekule, the German chemist, conceived the atomic arrangement of molecules in a single dream. Even certain logical determinations of my own developed in this paper were formulated during REM periods. Practically everyone can remember some dream where there was involved a reasoning process; perhaps to the extent of taking an examination or playing chess.

A typical dream report using analytical thought comes from the archives of experimental studies (here the subject is dreaming of a theatrical production):

> I was walking behind the leading lady when she suddenly collapsed and water was dripping on her. I ran over to her and felt water dripping on my back and head. The roof was leaking. I was very puzzled why she fell down and decided some plaster must have fallen on her. I looked up and there was a hole in the roof. I dragged her over to the side of the stage and began pulling the curtains.

Here, then, is a series of logical determinations derived from reasoned response to dream stimuli. First, he apparently reasons from the water dripping that the roof must be leaking, as they are inside a theater. Next he analyzes the cause of her fall and determines that plaster must have dropped on her because of the leak. He looks up and sees a hole in the roof, verifying his assumption. Finally, implicitly reasoning that a dramatic presentation is in progress and people are watching, he drags her off and begins closing the curtains. In each step the dreamer functions as he would have done in a similar waking experience: stimuli, interpretation and response.

Various external implications of cortical interpretation arid discrimination of external stimuli during sleep and REM's have been collected from controlled experiments. Harold Williams (1963) showed that subjects who responded (.by pressing micro-switches taped to their hands) only very seldom to a tone stimulus presented during REM sleep under standard conditions were capable of much greater responsiveness when some special importance was attached to their noticing the tone. Then interpretive responses were comparable to that received during other EEG stages of light, low voltage sleep. Ian Oswald (1962) revealed that when playing a tape of many names to subjects in NREM 2 and 3, K complexes indicating responsiveness to external stimuli were significantly more frequent and better formed when the stimulus was the subjects own name than when it was the name of another person or even his own name said backwards. Li, Jaslper and Henderson (1952) reported that a narcoleptic patient of theirs could sleep through the noise made by the experimenters hitting a brass pail right beside the bed, but would awaken immediately if her own name was softly spoken.

In reviewing various experimental data Webb states, "There have been a number of experiments which have substantiated the recognized capacity of, for example, a mother's ability to respond to the least sound of her child while not responding to much more intense sounds and signals during the night. In one such experiment subjects were asked to respond by clinching their hands to their own name but not to other names when played in a tape during the night. They did so with considerable efficiency. In another study subjects were taught to respond to a tone within a given limit of time in order to avoid a shock. It was found that during sleep subjects could respond to the tone (and not respond to similar but different signals) without awakening. Also subjects that were told they would be paid if they awakened to correct sounds were able to 'collect' with remarkable efficiency." The evidence denotes some interpretive thinking process at work in both REM's and NREM sleep. Also, the dream reports given so far for both lucid and non-lucid conditions confirm a definite analytical function present during REM periods. Likewise, David Foulkes (1964) established similar logical processes existing in NREM sleep (although here the form is not so much stimulus—reasoned response but rather reflective or forward-looking thought).

Observing this continuity of interpretive and analytical systems throughout the SDW cycle Zvi Giora's hypothetical offering (*Am. Journal of Psychiatry*, 1972) seems appropriate for elucidation: "It is suggested that cognition does not change its function through the various states of mind but that its level of organization shifts from state to state."

This statement of Giora's might lend some intimation as to why, if analytical and cognitive forms of activity remain intact in dreams, do we rarely determine that we are dreaming and let the most bizarre and absurd contingencies pass as real events—a puzzle that has occupied much of my mental exercise over the past years. If cognition changes only its level of organization, not its function, then perhaps that level of organization is dependent not on some dynamic quality within the level but on extrinsic influences and reaction to them.

This would mean that in dreams cognition is reflective of the organizational particulars within the dream and not of waking-dream relationships; what is absurd in life is not necessarily absurd in dreams. Cognition does not change; only its level of sensory organizations. In other words, in early development the experience of REM dreams dictate to the young mind certain relationships between sundry aspects of dream events. These relationships, as strange as they may be in time, space, and form distortion become the norm for a small child incapable of determining their deviance from reality.

Only later as the child becomes aware of certain logical relationships of waking life does he learn to analyze and reason things to be correct in reality. He learns also that in order for things to be required of waking time-space absolutes there must exist a prior condition of consequential interaction. Usually waking up establishes this condition. The person knows that he has been asleep, and now that he is woken, things are expected to relate to one another in certain prescribed ways. The clock will advance forward in a predictable fashion. Turning on the coffee will result in a predetermined bubbling action, which in turn will be succeeded by a rise in temperature of the coffee. Pushing down the toast will be followed by an ordained ascension of the same toast within specific boundaries of time; and so forth. His cognition responds accordingly, adjusting itself to the interaction of waking events. If any of the aforementioned resultants fail to appear a logical waking cause will be sought for and found; very rarely will the reality of the situation be questioned.

When the individual goes to sleep, his cognition prepares itself for a new time-space continuum. So when the condition of dream interrelationship develops the cognition accepts things on an organizational level relative to consequence in the dream state (a level that is the true normal level since it was the original level of human existence). Thus dream events are not judged by waking standards but by the persons own dream standards; and if some cause-effect relationship is antithetical to his organizational level then a "dream" reason will be sought for first and inspection of "reality" only as a last resort.

It is when this last resort is taken that lucid dreams can evolve. Something must violate the dream standards and leave the determination of the dream state (lucidity) as the only explanation. Such was the case in Fox's first "dream of knowledge" which was precipitated by the change of position of the pavement stones within the same dream. In Fox's dream cognitive organizational level the changing of the stones was a violation of established dream relationships of time and space and resulted in a critical attitude toward the "reality" of the event. Since everyone's dream world "realities" differ, there is no single contingency that would universally violate the dream systems and lead to critical inspection and analytical determination of lucidity. This process of cognitive organizational adjustment might provide, then, the answer to why so many weird and distorted things happen in dreams without a lucid revelation.

However, dream violation of its own organizational level is not the only method of lucid attainment through interpretive thought. The dreamer through the function of the cortex and its relation to the lower brain structures outlined earlier interprets external material as demonstrated by the stimuli—discriminative response experiments, and this can result in the determination of the dream state. In effect, this is what possibly happens many mornings upon awakening from a REM period (or NREM for that matter). The dreamer receives the incoming impressions of external stimuli of, for example, a radio alarm clock; interprets what they mean; determines it means he is dreaming and must wake up; and does so by cortical signaling of the reticular formation. If. the alarm is not meant for him he will probably determine such and remain asleep. This process of stimuli evaluation, however, is so rapid that it is rarely remembered upon awakening. (Note: a loud alarm will produce direct facilitation of the reticular formation without cortical action).

One method by which this process of external analysis is done has been illustrated by experiments in dream incorporation of stimuli. The impression is often incorporated into the ongoing dream event and interpreted for its associative meaning. In one such study Ralph Berger (UCLA, 1963) found a definite connection between stimulus and subsequent retrieved dream content about 50% of the time depending on the meaningfulness of the stimulus. Mardi Horowitz (Image Formation and Cognition, 1970) remarks on the subject: "Dream investigators have stimulated volunteers during dreaming sleep with lights, sounds, or temperature changes. The stimulus was clearly incorporated in 20 to 60% of the dreams in one study of Dement and Wolpert (1958). When an external stimulus is incorporated into a dream, it is often changed symbolically and incorporated into the ongoing dream fantasy."

A dream report evoked by using experimental stimuli (Rechtschaffen et. al., 1963) displays how the cortex might interpret incoming impulses during dreams. Here 67 seconds after the subject showed a slight body movement, a 500 cps. tone was presented below the waking threshold for seven seconds. This was followed in turn by 27 seconds of no stimulation, a second presentation of the tone, and an additional 32 seconds of no stimulation. Then the subject was awakened by a loud buzzer. He reported that he dreamt he was standing on a rock talking with someone, then:

> ...a little whistling tone was going on...and then it went off. And (the other person) said 'Oh, you had better get this over quickly, because you may have to wake up soon...' I just said 'Oh' to this and I think I heard the whistling tone again...Then the same scene was there for some time, and I was just walking around trying to think of what was going on.

Here the tone enters the dream from no specific meaning-associated source. The cortex tries to analyze the tone and in doing so manifests some of its thoughts in the dream body of the other person (that the tone might be some kind of alarm to wake up). It comes to no conclusion and the primary perceptual character (himself) continues to try to decipher its meaning (through cortical direction). If given time he might have come to a lucid determination.

Dream incorporation and subsequent perceptual response is not, however, the only form of cortical analysis and discrimination of the external environment. As in waking, certain mental processes of information filtering continue outside the conscious attention of the person. The information is sorted as to value and possible importance before the selected impulses are manifested into the hallucinatory drama. This function would account for why not all material is incorporated in experimental subjects and why the meaningfulness of the stimuli has been shown to be a factor in the rate of incorporation.

Lucid dreams, therefore, can result from two possibilities: violation of one's dream cognitive organizational level and interpretation of external impulse through response to selected incorporated stimuli.

Most initial encounters with lucidity result, as in my own and Fox's case as well as the majority of those researched by Miss Green, from dream violation (recurrent nightmares, incongruity, etc.). However, both close reading of dream reports of habitual lucid dreamers and the preponderance of lucid dreams during morning hours where external stimuli is greatest, reveal the likelihood of incorporation analysis as the primary factor in mature lucid revelations. Perhaps Green's fourth causal agent, "recognition of dreamlike quality of the experience," is nothing more than a rapid interpretation and determination of external influences such as noise, light, bodily sensations, etc.

An example of lucidity resulting from incorporation and reasoned response comes from my own diary:

> I was sleeping at my father's house on the living room davenport late Sunday morning, dreaming of playing basketball outside with some friends. In the kitchen a few feet away my step-mother was frying bacon in the skillet for the large family; and both the sound and smell of the bacon was filling the living room. These sensory impressions entered my dream in the form of two boys frying bacon over a stick fire next to the basketball court. I stopped playing and walked over to them and told them how good the bacon sounded and smelled and how hungry I was. They said I couldn't have any because we wouldn't let them play basketball. So I stood there watching and began to think about how my step-mother always cooked bacon on Sunday morning. Then I began to wonder if this was Sunday so that I might be able to have some; which in turn made me think that if it was, this bacon on the fire might be a dream of the real bacon in the kitchen; which made me look around and determine that the whole thing was indeed a dream and I could continue it into one of my extended lucid adventures—which I did, but not for long as I was awakened by my step-mother for breakfast (an interruption not altogether unpleasant).

While such critical inspection of the dream event from either violation of relationships or stimuli interpretation of incorporated impressions may result in determination of a dreaming condition, it does not always do so. Many times a dreamer might question the situation and wonder if he is dreaming and logically determines he is not (when he really is). Green quotes several cases of such analysis and "reality" decisions. Two subjects report as follows:

There were times when I argued with myself about whether I was dreaming or not—saying it is O.K., it is only a dream—and then saying to myself 'no it is not…this is reality.

I certainly have had dreams in which I distinctly remember asking myself the question, 'Am I dreaming? This occurs quite often—perhaps as much as once a week. However, as far as I can remember, the vast majority of the time the question was either left unanswered in my mind or was answered in the negative, and the dream continued without the thought returning to me.

From my own accounts:

I was dreaming I was in a fight with a much bigger person than myself. I realized I was dreaming because the same thing had happened many times before in dreams (recurrent nightmares). I said to the other person "You don't have a chance. This is all taking place in a dream of mine and you can't win. Want to quit?" He replied, "Oh yes, that's what you think; let's find out." And he started to push me. I thought to myself, "This seems terribly real. What if it isn't a dream?' I decided it wasn't and ran away (as I have a penchant to do under such circumstances).

One additional occasion of dream experience that usually evokes critical examination of the dream and lucidity must be mentioned. This is a condition known through esoteric dream circles as a "false awakening", or a dream of waking up from a dream (probably caused by cortical interpretation and imitation of external sensations). These false awakenings happen to lucid and ordinary dreamers alike. An example might be dreaming you get up and get a drink of water and then waking up for real and realizing the first awakening was a dream (false). Such "false awakenings" represent a special interest for the dream investigator as they provide the easiest method for lucid determinations. This is because by dreaming he wakes up and is at home in bed the dreamer establishes a waking cognitive organizational level and things will be expected to relate in the manner they have taken in previous waking life. Thus critical awareness is not dependant on either violation of dream relationships or evaluation of incorporated stimuli but can arise from events breaking waking standards. The littlest deviation from the waking norm can result in arousal of the critical faculty.

For a documented example:

Twice or more during childhood I remember apparently awakening from a dream and discovering that I had not done so because I could not turn on the light…I recognized in the dream that I was still asleep (because of my being unable to turn on the light) and made a great effort to shout and wake myself up properly.

And another:

> I dreamt I was dreaming and then woke up and sat up in bed and saw the room around me. However, after a time—a matter of a half minute or so—I realized I was dreaming that I was awake, and this resulted in me actually waking up.

Possibly this tendency to awaken after dream awareness, as suggested earlier, is due to the cortex functioning in its usual manner after such awareness as a result of waking—associated stimuli. The cortex signals the reticular formation to reinforce or replicate external impulses causing arousal. However, through the same fashion by concentrating attention on dream stimuli the cortex can signal the reticular formation to replicate such dream impulses causing the hallucination to increase in vividness and intensity and allowing the conscious to remain in the dream until waking is desired.

Hopefully, for the sake of lucid experience, the dreamer will critically examine his dream world, decide he is dreaming, not wake up, and have an extended lucid adventure. Yet, one does not have to wait for some fortuitous incongruity or stimulus interpretation to tell him he is in position for lucidity. As will be demonstrated in the next section certain teaching or training methods can be employed using experimentally induced dream violation and signal-associated incorporation to offer lucid dreams to most anyone who wants them.

NOTES ON PART V

1. Many times the imaginative faculties in a dream will attempt to create an acceptable answer to an apparent violation of the person's dream realities. In such, a case the question "Am I dreaming?" will never arise—there is no reason it should. An instance of this happening in my own experience started with a dream about my being in the army reserve and we. were called to active duty. This apparently was an inchoate violation of my dream would as I began to explain to another soldier that all this was very strange since I had always hated the military and could not even remember enlisting. To be sure, this was the cognitive groundwork for a lucid realization; but in this case it didn't come off. The innovative screenwriters of the mind immediately began working to "patch, up" the dream and consequently I was told by the fellow, soldier that I was lucky I had only joined the reserves; provisionally to obtain material for a book and I could leave anytime I wanted. This, of course, satisfied me and prevented my questioning the reality of the situation and having a lucid determination.

The process of such dream "improvisation" would naturally be somewhat abstruse and operates in that obscure region of the mind we define as "creative." However, the presence of a mechanism, that serves to correct mistakes in the dream, organization does not necessarily mean that the mind wishes to prevent any lucid epiphanies nor does, it destroy the *raison d'etre* for lucid dreams that we have been developing here. Rather, it merely shows that in the dream world as in the waking one the mind seeks the easiest answer to a question;, and it always seems easier to "cover" a few gaps in a story than doubt the whole setup.

2. The false awakening is of particular interest to occultists as it presents a unique situation of physical-astral opportunities. Presumably, a person in the false awakening state has entered a condition different from dreaming, a condition where consciousness is awake and viewing the actual world—not a hallucinatory one, and the body is asleep in a sort of catatonic state. To project the astral body, all one need do is step out of the physical body and the two become separated (although connected by some sort of silver life-force cord). In this event, it is possible to look back front the astral body and see ones own physical form still asleep on the bed. This duality is referred to as the "Double" in Castenada's *Tales of Power* and it offers limitless possibilities of extrasensory awareness-and discovery. Fox maintains that in this astral state, all time—past, present and future—exists simultaneously and that one can encounter people and objects that existed hundreds of years ago or have yet to be created.

From the standpoint of this paper, the false awakening, because it is a fairly frequent and normal occurrence, becomes a useful method for lucid initiation. If every time we believe we wake up, we were to attempt walking through a wall or some similar test, it could be easily determined if we were really awake or only dreaming of being awake.

PART VI:
EXPERIMENTAL LUCIDITY

As a way of precaution lest this paper be taken for some semblance of scientific methodology I emphasize that the material presented in this section is largely observations and deductions from my own rather barbaric procedures. Because of my failure to uncover in my readings any systematic or experimental attempts to initiate lucidity in subjects other than Green's interest aroused lucid dreams in two individuals, and also by reason of the limited capacities of my equipment, finances, and academic standing I am prohibited from the utilization of any true laboratory techniques and can only approach those techniques with parallel but less controlled and therefore less reliable methods. I will, however, where possible corroborate my findings with related if not identical experimentation of others.

My own research revolved around four principal methods for lucid arousal: a. suggestion b. acquired habit of inspection c. associative signaling, and d. conditioned learning (I did not employ interest initiation of lucidity as such method has been reasonably established as viable by Green—interest initiation being lucid dreams developing from mere interest in the subject and reading of dream accounts of other lucid travelers).

a. While I was prevented from use of hypnotic suggestion due to lack of professional requirements I did attempt both pre-sleep and during-sleep taped suggestion as a way of lucid training. Prior to the presentation of such attempts it will do here to refer to documented use of hypnosis for dream content control and certain unique relationships between hypnotic sleep and spontaneous lucid dreams as a background for my own work with casual suggestion.

Concerning the influencing of dream content through hypnotic suggestion J.M. Stoyva (1965), employing the EEG/REM method of eliciting dream content, found seven of sixteen subjects almost invariably (70-100% of the time) produced content reports in accord with pre-sleep suggestions given by the experimenter while the subject was in a hypnotic trance. Data from another study (C.T. Tart, 1964) on the effect of direct hypnotic suggestion also exhibits that dream content can be influenced by such: five of ten subjects reported dreams in accord with suggestions. Earlier, 1963, Tart found that not only content but behavioral aspects such as awakening could be controlled by hypnosis. By using posthypnotic suggestion subjects could be made to awaken at either the beginning or end of their stage 1 dreams.

If subject dreams can be affected by hypnotic suggestion along with the SDW cycle and its controlling mechanisms then why not perceptual dream thought processes? Possibly a hypnotic order to become aware of the dream condition at some specific time or as a reaction to certain suggested content material would result in lucid determination.

Celia Green draws some causal relationships between lucid dreams and hypnosis although she does not prescribe actual lucid initiation from hypnotic direction. Instead she reflects that for one reason or another while under hypnosis subjects have experienced spontaneous lucid dreams without being told to do so. It is difficult to say why spontaneous lucidity should arise of hypnotic states. One answer might be that the hypnotist's suggestion does not coincide with the dreamer's cognitive level of organization. In other words since the hypnotist could not know the framework of the subjects dream or hypnotic world his suggestion might have been an unnatural development for it and such violation of its standards of time-space relationships precipitated lucidity.

Naturally, casual suggestion cannot be expected to be as effective in influencing dream and sleep behavior but it can lend limited results. In experiments conducted by Frobenias (1927) it was discovered that subjects given pre-sleep suggestion can wake from sleep at a randomly pre-selected target on most attempts. His subjects usually awoke within 10 minutes of the selected time. Elder (1941) confirmed these results.

In my own experimentation with lucid evocation through suggestion, I had five subjects listen to a tape recording for fifteen minutes before sleep. The tape repeated "You will dream you are at a dance; the people have no faces, so you realize you are dreaming." This was tried for three consecutive nights. The following mornings yielded dream reports containing an element of dancing in two subjects but neither revealed any lucid revelations. However, when the tape was played continuously throughout the night the reports showed that three dreamt of a dance and one achieved limited lucidity. He said that in the dream he had thought, "This must be a dream," but woke up right after and couldn't remember what made him determine he was dreaming. No reports displayed the presence of people without faces (not necessarily indicating the absence of such content but possibly the forgetting of it during the night or upon awakening).

Acquired habit of inspection is a process by which environmental inspection becomes so automatic that it carries over into all levels of cognition. Concerning other forms of habitual behavior during sleep as corroborative material Renneker (1952) reports on a patient who habitually awoke a few moments before the alarm was to go off. Omwake and Loranz (1933) arid Brush (1930) also offer data that leaves little doubt that some subjects can awake at a preset time due to habit.

In my investigation the object was to have the subjects consciously inspect the waking environment every five minutes in hopes that this would habitually carry over into dream behavior. Three subjects attempted such tedious inspection at five minute intervals for three days. The results were somewhat less than encouraging. Only one reported critically inspecting his dream milieu and probably because it became so automatic to inspect and reaffirm being awake he observed his dream world and determined that it was real as perfunctorily as he had during the day.

Obviously these first two methods are not overly effective at arousing lucidity in subjects; but they do suggest that if continued long enough with enough interest such a result can be obtained; as hopefully it has been demonstrated that external techniques can indeed influence both dream material and perceptual thought processes which, of course, are the stuff that lucid dreams are made of.

As mentioned earlier, content dream violation of the individuals cognitive level of organization as was attempted experimentally with the taped suggestion is one of two normal processes of lucid determination. The other is interpretation of incorporated stimuli; and this is the premise of my latter two methods. Here an attempt will be made to introduce meaning-associated stimuli into the dream and thereby induce cortical perceptual analysis and lucidity.

Associative signaling was employed using a muffled bell alarm (by taping the hammer) and pre-sleep instructions to three subjects. The desire was for the alarm to be incorporated into a dream and interpreted for its lucid-related signal as instructed. In the same manner that the morning alarm might enter the dream and be interpreted to mean "I am sleeping, the sound means I am to awake"; the muffled bell alarm signals, "I am dreaming, the sound means I am to have a lucid dream." (While not mentioning lucid evocation, Tart (1965) speculated on such incorporation signaling: "Can subjects learn to incorporate some stimuli effectively enough so that one could use these stimuli as signals to indicate to the subject that he should carry out a specific action, for example, dream about a particular topic or carry out some motor act.") The bell was set and reset to ring at intervals corresponding to the normal pattern of EEG stage 1 REM. (Since this pattern is not fixed either in appearance or duration there was considerable room for error in "hitting" dream periods.) Also the clock was taped to the subjects' hands and he was told to push the alarm shut-off when the bell rang without waking once he has responded to the signal. The purpose of this was both to indicate that he had interpreted the bell and to prevent the continued ringing from aborting a possible lucid dream through cortical-reticular aggravation. Then five minutes after the bell the subjects were awakened.

Notwithstanding these parochial devices, the results were relatively favorable; after three nights of use two subjects were pushing the shut-off without awakening and one reported dream content with a manifest element of a bell sound. By the fifth night all three were stopping the alarm without awakening and two had reported dreams with bell incorporation. Also one remembered thinking in his dream that the bell was a signal that he was dreaming but couldn't recall what happened after that. After one week of testing two subjects were using the bell as a signal to inspect the dream situation and one reported a lucid determination followed by a well defined lucid dream extending until I woke him.

A more sophisticated method of external stimulus incorporation and perceptual response was developed using theories of classical conditioning and a home-made REM apparatus. I made the REM device or rather EMP (eye movement per minute) machine using a clock with a second hand, two battery operated binary counters from the local electronics merchant, a hand button, and an eye switch of two copper strips designed to measure the difference in protrusion between the cornea and its ambient areas. Eye movement would open and close the electrical circuit causing the binary counter to record such action. The second hand on the clock was connected so as to reset the counter to zero every minute. Then a light was set up to go on upon a specific binary read-out and this was taped to the subjects other eye. So when a certain number of eye movements per minute appeared indicating a dreaming condition (as the number of such movements is significantly higher during REM periods than NREM it was not difficult to determine the point of REM onset) the bright light went on over the subjects eye and could only be shut off or prevented by pushing a button taped to his hand. By avoidance reaction it was hoped to teach the subject to realize when he was starting to dream without the light and for this realization to enter the dream in the form of perceptual lucidity.

A similar experiment used in connection with EEG discrimination in subjects instead of lucid dreams was reported in *Current Research on Sleep and Dreams*, 1966. Here subjects were trained to push a button in order to avoid a shock that was set to go off near the beginning of EEG stage 1 REM. The results proved that subjects could learn to discriminate between the various EEG stages and push the button prior to the shock, and at times even before the EEG pattern recorded stage 1 waves; suggesting that they knew not only when they were dreaming but also when they were about to dream. While the potential for possible lucid dreams after such discrimination was not pursued the experiment does support both the existence of interpretive thought in sleep and dreams and the feasibility of using external teaching techniques for lucid instruction.

Here are the results of my own study with three subjects: by the second night of experimentation two of the subjects were pressing the button after the light went on without awakening and, upon our awakening, one reported a dream involving "a blinding sun." After three nights all three were pressing the button after the light without awakening but still only one reported dreams with light incorporation. By the fifth night one subject began pressing the button before the light; however upon our awakening him he could not remember doing so. After six nights of REM use two of the subjects were pressing the button before the light and one reported thinking in the dream "I am dreaming, that light is coming," but failed to hold the dream or preserve lucidity. The following night this subject did not remember any lucid determinations but the other two, both of whom were responding prior to the light, each reported dream thought content that revealed a realization of the dream state and one was able to hold the scene and awareness through concentration. He relates:

> I was dreaming I was swimming somewhere in a big lake. I felt like something was going to happen and looked up into the sky. I remembered something about a bright light and then realized that I must be dreaming because the light was going to start and I had to shut it off. I don't remember actually turning it off but I must have since it never appeared. I started to wake up but told myself, 'You are supposed to stay asleep and have one of those special dreams', so I concentrated on looking at the fading scene of the lake and it became more distinct and I remained asleep. All I remember is just standing there looking at the lake and being surprised how real it looked for being a dream lake and almost started thinking that it was real and maybe I was really awake when you woke me up.

It goes without saying that these preceding experiments are considerably less than controlled investigations. Both the equipment and the methods permit of egregious violations of accuracy and reliability. And yet the very presence of such "unfinished" techniques proposes two observations for the sanguine minded individual. First, if such limited experimentation can yield results in confirmation of the ability to learn lucid dreaming then, surely, professional laboratory study would achieve that much more. And second, since only simple materials and determination were here required to initiate lucid dreams, such initiation is not dependent on complicated electronic provisions but can be produced using easily obtainable items and layman know-how. My presumptuous REM device cost a total of about ten dollars, the bell alarm for associative signaling, $2.50.

If anything, my experimentation suggests the possibility of extending the lucid experience to almost anyone and refutes allegations that lucid dreams are paranormal events encountered only by "gifted" individuals." What it does not do is determine if such universal lucidity is good or bad. Even if dreams possess no psychologically medicinal requirement the promulgation of "dreams of knowledge" to the populace is of no more than conjecturable value. There is a long way to go before a "dream machine" becomes the advertised special of some "five and ten."

Whatever.

Next I will discuss various aspects of dreams relevant to this paper, and then present briefly certain therapeutic potentials of lucid dreams, followed by a psychic personal note; and I hope to wrap this thing up before too long.

NOTES ON PART VI

1. The manner in which interest in lucid dreams can serve as an aid in having them is similar to the way in which interest in any subject motivates a constant involvement with the subject. In other words, if a person is sincerely interested in a topic that topic appears continuously in his conversations and thoughts; and if that topic is lucid dreams and if the appearance happens itself to be in the conversations and thoughts of a dream then dream inspection and lucid determination might well occur. As an example, in a recent dream of mine I was at a religious revival meeting and the speaker was talking about miracles and the audience seemed skeptical about the existence of divine miracles in the modern world. I began thinking about how great it would be if this were a dream and I could fly up in the air and vanish in smoke in front of everyone. This thought in turn made me decide to inspect the scene to determine if it might indeed be but a dream; which I decided it was and proceeded to carry out my own miracle. Needless to say the people in the dream were considerably impressed with my performance.

It is probable that if lucidity should ever become a frequent and universal condition of normal dreaming throughout the world it would do so by and large through mass interest initiation—at least as far as newly arriving generations are concerned. As children are raised, they would be encouraged to discuss, write down, and concern themselves with their dreams in all phases of life. They would be told of the meaning and possibilities of lucid dreams and instructed to always observe both the waking and dream worlds so that if they are dreaming they may be aware of it.

2. A good case for the feasibility of lucid inculcation rests in a study by Kilton Steward in Tart's *Altered States Of Consciousness*. In his investigations of the Senoi tribe of Malaysia he found that from a very young age the children seem to have a rudimentary form of "dreams of knowledge" They are taught to be aware of their dreaming condition so that they may combat without fear the evil forces that appear in dreams and also may learn from the good forces. When the Senoi children have nightmares they are not afraid but call on the other dream people to help them fight off whatever is threatening them. When they meet a good "spirit" they ask it for a song or dance that they might relate to the tribe when awake. Each morning the tribe gathers to discuss everyone's dream and what it might mean. The Senoi child speaks and thinks "dreams" all day and consequently this

interest carries over into the speaking and thinking of REM sleep and enables lucid awareness to occur.

In our society, however, the importance of dreams has become relegated to mere conversation piece or psychoanalytic reflection and the lucid potential ignored. Children are not encouraged to discuss or record dreams and if perchance a child has a dream where he knows that he is dreaming he usually wakes up because he does not understand what is happening and becomes afraid. Upon awakening he either forgets it or dismisses it as a freakish or "unnatural" event and does not tell anyone for fear of being labeled "abnormal." If he should perhaps tell his parents or some other adult he would probably be told that one should not be aware in a dream; that people are not meant to control their dream world; that if man becomes a god of his own universe he would do terrible and immoral things because nobody could stop or punish him; that if he continued in such a dream he might not be able to wake up; and so on *ad nauseum*. By adulthood dreams become an insignificant part of life and awareness an insignificant part of dreams. There you have it.

PART VII:
ASPECTS OF DREAMS AND DREAMING

A common remark made of dreams is that they are rarely remembered. It seems that only nightmares or dreams occurring immediately before awakening are recalled. Wolpert and Trosman (1958) write that although dreams were reported by 80 to 90% of subjects when they were awakened during a dream period, such an awakening five minutes after a dream period results in only fragmentary recall in 5 to 10% of the subjects. Recall after ten minutes was quite rare.

I consider there to be two possible reasons for this tendency to forget dreams. First, it is conceivable that dreams are forgotten, at least as far as the waking consciousness is concerned, for the same reason that the incidental filler of the day is: lack of intensity of stimuli and reticular reinforcement. Taking two scientific verities: that the number of nerve impulses for a given stimulus is proportional to the intensity of the stimulus (Halden K. Hartline, 1934),(Adrian, 1932); and that reticular replication in waking due to conscious attention increases that number of impulses; and using the theoretical relationships of impulse and RNA base formation (one to one) and RNA to memory; this might mean in terms of dreams that the intensity of dream images is not sufficient in respect to impulses to form strong memory traces through multiple base synthesis. Only in reticular facilitation due to emotional stress in nightmares or repetitive reinforcement upon waking recall immediately after REM periods can dreams be remembered. This might also account for why incidental, waking material (day residue) can become a salient feature of dreams (Foulkes, *Psychology of Sleep*, 1966) and why sensory information can be remembered in dreams that does not register in waking perception (Poetzl, 1960). Dream images, perhaps, are all composed of identical low impulse transfers. Consequently all memory traces have "equal time" during dreaming whereas in waking the weaker traces have to compete with the stronger for conscious reflection.

Another possible reason for the inability to remember those dreams which occur within REM periods followed by NREM sleep rather than awakening might be that the coded RNA units formed during the dream are disassociated during the ensuing sleep process before the necessary protein for memory consolidation can be synthesized from them. Some evidence supports the beliefs that memory traces take a certain amount of time to consolidate (Zinkin, 1965), (Broadbent, 1958), (Cronholm and Mollander, 1957, 1958). This time might be that required to form protein from RNA definition. Therefore, the breakdown of RNA for ATP before protein formation is completed would result in an absent or incomplete memory of dream experience.

More important than dream recall in the mental occupations of theorists has been the subject of dream content and development. While it is beyond the scope and design of this paper to formulate any extended hypothesis on this subject (a valuable one can be found in *Dreams and the Growth of Personality*, 1972, by Ernest Rossi), a cursory outline of my own conceptions will be offered here.

I observe five primary factors in dream content and development: personality influences (drive expression, compensation, etc.), imaginative memory processes, interpretation and incorporation of external stimuli, inherited memory factors, and interpretive response to dream situation.

The personality factors that influence dream content have, of course, received considerable attention. It is probable that all of the various mechanisms introduced by Freud, Jung, Adler, Pearls, Fromm, etc. are active in dreams. How they develop, however, remains largely unanswered. Foulkes (1964) maintains that dream framework does not present itself spontaneously in a dream but instead develops continuously throughout the night both in earlier dreams and NREM sleep periods where thought processes similar to waking cognition reveal elements later manifested in REM dreaming. Personality mechanisms then, operate within a larger system of sleep-dream patterns connected by a continuous process of interrelated thought. Rechtschaffen, Vogel and Shaikun (1963) put it a little better than I: "dreams do not arise *sui generis* as psychologically isolated mental productions but emerge as the most vivid and memorable part of a larger fabric of interwoven mental activity during sleep." Dissecting these definitions, an important contribution to lucid theory is exposed. For if dreams compose only one facet of a continuous process of cognition throughout the sleep-dream cycle then it is unlikely that the logical and waking-like thought functions present in pre-REM and necessary for lucidity would be eradicated at dream onset and leave the continuity of remaining mental activity intact.

Imaginative memory processes would include both day residue and natural imaginative associations from them and other dream content. One particular dream image or event evokes an associated past image or event which is manifested through an imaginative elaboration of it consistent with the dream scheme. In some ways this would work in an analogous manner to daydreaming. One example that might show such a process is taken from Horowitz's *Image Formation and Cognition*:

> I was riding with a guy on the back of the motorcycle. I was in my new blue dress; he was dressed all in black. Then suddenly we were sitting in my back yard eating a lot of stuff spread out on a blanket. In the next scene there was a bunch of letters on a sign...

Here the black clothing reminds her of a blanket and the "stuff" on the blanket background is imaginatively associated with letters on a sign.

In laboratory research, Foulkes writes, "Rechtschaffen and I found a positive relationship between imagination judged in a waking test of fantasy, the Thematic Apperception Test and both the presence of dream recall on REM sleep awakening and the rated imaginativeness of the elicited REM reports."

While Foulkes' statement requires qualification in that it was not used in this context of dream development, it might provide insight into the similarity of imaginative memory mechanisms in waking "dreaming" and REM dreaming.

Interpretation of external impressions would consist of the methods already outlined of stimuli incorporation and interpretive constructions built upon them. In the instance of the dream material about the tone incorporation (Part 5) the interpretation of the tone produced a dream development utilizing it as a content factor. Foulkes points out that an externally suggested name such as "Gillian", for example, produces a dream element of a woman from Chile (Chilean). This was dream content derived from an associative interpretation of the word "Gillian."

The precise placement of inherited memory functions in dream design is difficult. Conceivably they would operate in accord with normal memory evocation. Let it suffice to say that given the theoretical nature of DNA-RNA-protein REM stimulation in neonates stored genetic memory traces might become a permanent fixture in the cortex along with experiential traces and work in the same manner as other low-impulse memory associations.

Interpretive response to dream stimuli involves the more reasoned and volitional agents of dream content. The dreamer acts according to the action alternatives presented to the perceptual body in the dream. His action response naturally affects the subsequent dream development. It may either be in the form of imaginative imitation of supposed result (e.g. a man dreams he is on a ship that is sinking, decides to jump, and the dream scene changes to water level through imaginative construction) or the interpretive response might be in the form of memory evocation of associated past events. Supportive of this is investigation done by Penfield (1958). Working with electrical stimulation of the brain, he found that stimulation of the temporal cortex produced flash backs of past life. He comments, "the psychical or interpretive area of the temporal cortex produced recall of past experiences or illusion of interpretation by conduction to some distant zone such as the hippocampus." Perhaps such a temporal/hippocampus (image formation) illusionary relationship exists in dreams during stimuli interpretation and response.

Oh well. That is my theory on dream content and development. Of course, lucid determination would seem to change that some. But not necessarily. Using only passive lucid observation, the proposed factors of dream development would evolve in their normal fashion (except maybe dream situation response—the man on the ship might not jump knowing it is only a dream). Without a doubt, conscious dream control like walking through walls or manipulation of hallucinatory objects would tend to affect dream development. However, in so far as my own experience has shown, lucid content control and the aforementioned content determinants are not antipathetic but can exist in mutual influence to one another: manipulation altering dream content and development and determinants vitiating lucid control.

The possible therapeutic value of both passive observation and dream control of lucidity and certain extra sensory notes are the subject of this last section. Coming up.

NOTES ON PART VII

1. It is also possible that dream forgetfulness occurs because of the shift in the organizational level of conscious sensory acceptance after waking. The person can remember certain primary images or events of the dream but cannot recall either why they occurred or the sequence of the action. This is because the waking conscious has no system of handling the time-space relationships of dreams. Once it begins adjusting to the organization of the "real" world the dream developments become vague because they possess no waking cause-effect relationship or sequential order from which they can be remembered. Normally during waking evocation of past events a person establishes a particular memory within an accustomed time-space continuum and proceeds sequentially to the desired event. For example: suppose you were asked to remember a high school dance. First, you would place yourself in the time and place of the dance; then approach the exact dance memory through the progression from one impression to its necessary sequel; then from these impressions to the next and finally arrive at the exact memory of the event. However, the time-space relationships of dreams do not permit of this waking process of memory and consequently dream development can only be remembered if a waking system of organizational, acceptance can be established in the dream as in lucid awareness.

However, it should be mentioned that a waking system of organizational acceptance of dream material does not necessarily follow a lucid determination. One may know he is dreaming in a specific part of a dream and still accept the larger dream framework as real. In this case the organizational acceptance of material would be that of the larger framework. For example, suppose a person has a dream about being in a war and in the dream he lays down to catch some sleep. Then a new dream begins within the other and involves a scene inside a theater. Now, if for one reason or another the dreamer has a lucid revelation, he may consider the theater to be chimerical and a dream, but still believe that the dream is taking place while he is actually sleeping on a cot in the middle of a war. He does not question the larger dream framework of the war—only the inner dream of the theater. Consequently, his "realities" and organizational acceptance of events within the lucid dream taking place in the theater will be determined by the relationships established in the war dream; and whereas these relationships are still of a non-waking time-space system, the lucid dream will be largely forgotten.

PART VIII:
LUCID OPPORTUNITIES, OR
I DO BELIEVE IN GHOSTS

The immediate reaction upon the realization in a dream that one is dreaming is an overpowering sensation of freedom and power. At the risk of surfeit I cannot stress this enough. The feeling is euphoric to say the least. And why not, self apotheosis would naturally instill a sense of omnipotence in a person.

It follows, then, that wish fulfillment is the initial activity of an enlightened dreamer and should be of fundamental interest to the therapist—out and out wish fulfillment (no need for Freudian distortion by reason of "super ego" acceptance of the dream state as in daydreaming). To fly, deny physical boundaries, make love, travel, astound dream people with feats of daring; this is all good stuff and enormously anxiety relieving and tension-mollifying. Working with dream content control using methods other than lucid direction it was reported in the *Journal of Abnormal Psychology* (v. 76 Oct. 1970) that such control may have important therapeutic and growth applications. Considering the much more volitional control of lucidity it follows that the therapeutic and growth potential of lucid dreams is enormous.

Yet the value of lucid dreaming does not end here, it begins. More important than wish fulfillment as far as clinical or salutary use is concerned is the application of passive lucidity for self discovery and personality development. If dreams are the manifest mental productions of both the psyche and its memory constituents, then aware observation of them can yield a knowledge not only of ones inner most self, but through the inherited traces, a discovery of one's cumulative psychological formation over the ages. No psychoanalyst could come close to that.

My qualifications to explore the potential therapeutic implications of lucidity end here at general speculation. And yet a note of caution is required. Lucid dreams are serious business despite my sometimes cavalier attitude in this composition. There are foreseeable drawbacks that must be reckoned with before a clinical or mental hygiene green light is given. While I have not encountered any of these nor have I read of any, they deserve mention. First, it is not without practical or professional foundation that when someone enjoys something considerably he doesn't easily give it up. What if lucid dreams should become a defensive escape world wherein an individual learns to hide from waking problems—a world where he is the king as opposed to one where he might be merely a pawn? And also what if the ability to determine dream world from waking world should vanish? As in accounts of pre-lucid dreams where persons logically and consciously inspect the dream environment and decide it is real, is it not possible to consciously analyze the waking world and determine it is a dream—visions of people jumping off buildings and such?

In any case, these warnings aside, my interest and abilities with the lucid phenomenon conclude here with the theoretical exercises given. As a psychic by-line before closing, however, I would like to make it clear that in no way did I intend to disparage the para-psychological enthusiasts who look toward evidence of ESP and mental separation in lucid dreams. In the course of my own association with the event I experienced many "happenings" which challenge scientific explanation. One such precipitated my experimentation with "astral projection" during the lucid condition:

> I had a lucid determination and a false awakening. Decided to walk downtown and see what adventures awaited me in my dream state. I decided to enter a gift shop that I had never been inside of during waking life as it had just recently opened; went in and looked around. On the wall in the back of the store something caught my attention—a sack of a specific type of plastic cowboys and horses that I had played with as a child but had never seen since in any toy shop. I awoke soon after and forgot about the dream in the days that followed. About a week later I had occasion to be in the store with a friend, and upon looking on the back wall noticed a plastic bag of toy cowboys and horses identical to those I had seen in my dream.

This, of course, brought back the memory of the lucid experience and strengthened my interest in the psychic nature of lucidity already aroused by Mr. Fox's accounts. Thereupon, for some time after, the occupation of my lucid time was spent experimenting with mind-body separation activities in an effort to prove the existence of astral projection. I will include two of the more provocative tests here.

Dec. 3, 1970: I had a lucid dream followed by a false awakening; maintained lucidity and decided to conduct a test. I got up (or dreamt I got up), walked through the wall into the kitchen to look at the wall clock; because I figured that if the clock was the same in my dream as after when I woke up that would prove I was traveling out of my physical body. I concentrated on the clock (of course if I was in an astral or ethereal condition I could not actually see the clock, only sense it) and determined it to read fifteen minutes until eleven. Then I walked back to my room, laid down, and woke up for real. I went in to check the clock and it read five minutes to nine. I took this as evidence that I was not projecting my mind but merely dreaming during the test. However, later in the day upon reflecting on the experiment I came to the following realization: In effect, fifteen to eleven and five to nine are the same, only the hands are reversed. A psychic pundit would argue that my ability to sense physical objects in the astral state did not extend to the minute difference between the lengths of the hands. I make no statement but at the very least, circumstance has once again acceded to the position of "coincidence extraordinaire."

May 5, 1972, I was living in an apartment with a friend and it was late in the morning. Had a lucid dream and willed the scene to change to my apartment; upon which I found myself laying on the bed, still dreaming. I decided to conduct an experiment so I got up and walked through the bedroom wall into the living room to record something that I could check upon awakening and which I had not seen the night before. Didn't notice anything that would work so went into the bathroom. On the shelf above the sink I saw a blue strip of what I sensed to be paper or cloth about two inches long. I went back to bed and awoke for real. When I went back in to the bathroom, I saw a torn-off blue jean belt loop that I never saw there before. Now if my friend had taken it off that morning before I got up that would prove I was astral traveling in the test. I called him at work but he couldn't remember if he had done so that morning or the night before.

So there you have it—subconscious recall of peripheral vision material or mind-body separation. Which is it?

These two experimental excerpts from my diary yield no evidence of either way. Yet they do lend an air of uncertainty to the use of the term "dream" to describe accurately lucid experience. I have only assumed such a definition for purposes of this paper and left the "supra-natural" aspects of lucidity to the parapsychologists. Perhaps I should have done the same for the psychologists.

Lucid dreams, whether "psyche" or psychic are an extraordinary and enigmatic phenomenon. Their true effect can only be felt first hand. It was attempted in this paper to bring this relatively unknown and unstudied experience into a proper perspective with both the occurrence and function of regular dreams and sleep and with the human personality. I intended neither to sell them nor initiate lucid proselytes. Nor do I intend to summarize here as summarization might seem to infer a total package, a neat explanation and prescription for lucid aware- ness. There is no such package and I am not the physician to prescribe. I do hope, though, that some of my hypotheses have seemed plausible, some suppositions and derivations correct. And I would desire enough credibility to incur academic inspection and further investigation-because the phenomenon, not I, really mer- its such consideration.

For, you see, lucid dreams do possess a potential, one hell of a potential, for change in the human mental and emotional existence. And change, after all, in man's life is what all the fuss is about.

NOTES ON PART VIII

1. This notion has been put somewhat figuratively. It is unlikely that one would witness a sequential depiction of his personality development proceeding nicely from archetypal to inherited to personal images. Rather, the point here is that lucid awareness has as its terrain all of the territory of memory occupied by genetic and acquired experience and an infinite variety of imaginative compositions. Observation and knowledge of the self is the purpose of such awareness; and while true understanding would require trained assistance in elaborating the meaning of various observations and discoveries, the opportunity of exploring the mind in lucid dreams exists as a monumental step forward in the search for the sources and reflections of human personality.

AFTERWORD: BETWEEN TWO WORLDS

Since the initial writing of this paper three years ago and its subsequent introduction in Dick McLeester's *Magic Theatre* book, it has been suggested to me by various readers that I follow up on the concept of dream organization or dream reality and its ramifications on psychological theory. I am told that I made loud noises about the effects of lucid dreams on behavioral study and then failed to elaborate on these effects. The case could be made for ignorance (an eminently justifiable position), or I might suggest I was employing the Ciceronian oratory technique of *sprezzatura* (a casual statement implying calamitous results); but if I remember correctly, the possibilities of the theoretical repercussions of lucidity and. levels of organizational or casual acceptance presented themselves to me as requiring much greater background knowledge then I had.

Such appears to have been the case and indeed still is. However, I have found it necessary to open up some sort of discussion on the extensions of a theory developed out of the existence of such things as lucid dreams, false awakenings, organizational levels, etc. This discussion will offer certain conceptual possibilities for consideration, each relating specifically to those areas of dream and waking experience that are concerned with the arrangement of stimuli as it appears to the conscious mind in the various states, In other words, the approach here is causal rather than interpretive. That is, the hypotheses presented here have their basis in the nature of causality and its interaction with the consciousness. This is not to be confused with mere physical causality; for although a rock thrown up in waking life must come down, the same rock in the dream world has many options, none of which necessarily violates any true law of causality. Causality in terms of this paper is simply the interrelationship of things. Fortunately, such an approach is possible in the light of recent investigations across the country like Henry Reed's Sundance Community Experiment which enable the inspection of dreams from standpoints independent of interpretive obligations,

In the main body of this paper I attempted to develop a continuous if somewhat tendentious explanation for various paradoxical elements of the mind during and after dreams. These elements were the integrity of analytical thought with only an occasional critical arousal; the higher occurrence of lucid dreams during the more realistic false awakenings; the learning nature of dream experience and yet the rapidity of dream forgetfulness after awakening; etc. The explanation offered was that there is more than one organizational level existing in the mind, and that the consciousness adjusts or misadjusts to different levels and accepts each according to its own indigenous interrelationships. Thus, for instance, the analytical processes rarely determine the dream experience to be unreal as the criteria for reality changes to those of the dream level of organization. At this time, however, I would like to define my understanding of the different levels in causal terms, substituting the phrase "causal system" for Giora's "level of organization" which was used originally in a context less phenomenological and more emotive in nature.

An inferential case for a separate dream causal system has already been made by other dream researchers in the course of their own pursuits. Both Celia Green and Patricia Garfield have suggested a dream "incongruity" as a possible initiator of a critical attitude toward the dream. They have pointed out that the incongruity is relative to normal dreams rather than waking life. However, "relative to normal dreams" implies that dreams have a norm and that the apparently chaotic and bizarre world of REM sleep actually has acceptable and unacceptable stimuli. Similarly, Ann Faraday in *The Dream Game* speaks of various time and space senses that accommodate themselves along top dog-bottom dog lines of experience; but time and space are but forms of interrelationship between things, and for the consciousness to vary in its sense or acceptance of these forms implies the existence of more than one system of interrelationships. In other words—if I may interpolate a philosophical dialectic—the presence of more than one a priori to sense of time and space which orders and determines reality necessitates the like presence of more than one reality.

Other theorists such as Ernest Rossi and James Donahue in *Dream Reality* have emphasized the flexible nature, of the consciousness in its relation to the involuntary aspects of dream experience. They each tend to support a view of the conscious perception as a vehicle of thought capable of adapting to different responses and expectations relative to dream material. This view would not be altogether inhospitable to an understanding of the consciousness as a perceptive instrument able to adjust its expectations and interpretations not only to the content of dream material but also to its arrangements.

It is always easy to make a case from components of others, and by some fast finger work appear to prove the composite. Yet, it is only fair to mention that while the ideas discussed might lend credence at least tangentially to a notion of causal systems or protean psyches, few contemporary investigators would view a theory which places the conscious mind in a position contingent to some sort of "dream physics' as anything but remotely plausible. Such limbs were never meant to hold.

Still, the argument could be made that a system of causality distinct from waking reality with an adjustable consciousness is the only explanation that could satisfy all the elements presented earlier. Yet to prove is not the intent. We would do better to accept the possibility of multiple causal systems and fill the confines of space here with a developmental scheme of how such a system evolves, how it interacts with waking experience, and how the conscious mind responds to and is affected by the systems' interaction.

In the earliest periods of experiential life, dream and waking phenomena are indistinguishable. As shown in Part 4, dream impulses follow the same neural-sensory tracts as normal environmental stimulation and are accepted by the cortex as coming from without. An immature brain has no way of differentiating between the "real" color red coming from electromagnetic sources and the chimerical red coming from psychophysical sources. The dream red, however, is capable of numerous imaginative reproductions or conditions, and because other stimuli will also begin appearing in dreams, the color red might become associated with various material and this association could develop into new content of specific arrangement. For example, the sound of a rattle, in dreams might be presented in a relationship to "red" and the two become associated if repeated to the extent that the consciousness begins to form an assumption or expectation of one when the other appears—it hears "rattle" when it sees red. Likewise, if the stimuli of "warm" should coincide with "rattle" then it is possible that an association of "warm" with "rattle," and as a consequence "warm" with "red" might form. "Red," then, could become causally associated with "warm"—the beginning of a causal system. Such dream causality, however, would not be rigid or consistent. The color red might also become imaginatively interrelated with other stimuli and many variations of content could result without necessarily upsetting the loosely developing "reality." The waking world at this time is just another variation of association of which the conscious mind is forming assumptions.

As an offspring of growing interrelationships between stimuli, the sense of time/space is emerging. This sense is merely the feeling of relationship, of causality, or more exactly, of separateness. There is no distinction between a sense of time and a sense of space—only a feeling of separateness between things, between "red" and "rattle," for instance. The polymorphous nature of dream experience prohibits any type of measurement to develop so that in most dreams the sense of separateness continues to be the only form of time/space interrelationship. In adult dreams this sense not only applies to individual stimuli but to events, settings, dream people and feelings of centrality (the "I" in dreams). We can feel that we are actively in the dreamland interacting with separate subjects: we pick things up, talk to "others," throw or catch, walk, etc. We can feel that we are in many objects simultaneously, and the sense of separateness changes. We can feel outside the dream, watching, but completely separate from what is happening. We might feel that two objects or two people or an object and a person are one—not separate, We might sense that many things, people, or places that in real life are divided widely by time and space have no feeling of separation.

It is perhaps this sense of time and space as separateness that Bertrand Russell has called "false memory" or the feeling of remembering something that never actually appeared phenomenological to the conscious—not the memory but the feeling of the memory. For example, suppose you dreamt that you were playing a football game and it was the second down with three yards to go. Now, although you didn't actually dream about the previous down, you would not normally wonder what happened to it but would instead feel that something happened separate of the second down.

As a child grows, however, his waking world begins to form certain interrelationships and associations that are not flexible but consistent. Sleep time starts to become mostly dark time. Balls always seem to roll and blocks do not. The kitchen stove is always "white" and "hot." Glass breaks, things fall "down," trees are connected to the ground, birds go with sky fish with water, dogs bark cats meow. Congruently, distance, form and interval begin replacing mere separateness; and slowly time and space become individual senses. The consciousness is starting to build assumptions about things that conflict with assumptions it already has. It sees that sometimes its body can jump off a step and only fall down but at other times float away. It becomes aware that at times places and people stay the same for specific periods and other times change in many ways. It finds that sometimes only one response will work, and at different times it can make many responses.

What is happening is that there are now two distinct causal systems developing, one of which has certain interrelationships—both physical and social—that tolerate little variation in response. For survival, the organism is forced to consciously adapt its acceptance, at least conditionally, to the waking world. However, the manner that this adaptation works varies in different cultures. In some societies like the Senoi tribe of Malaysia, the consciousness is inculcated to accept both systems according to the laws of waking organization. It learns to interpret and respond to both with a waking level of acceptance. It can distinguish between real and dream experience and acts with the awareness of its condition and position in time and space. It has, in short, a continuous lucid life in dreams. This does not mean that the Senoi see the dream world as false, but only as an alternate plane of existence with different possibilities. Both dream people and waking people are "real" and both must be treated alike. Behavior must be consistent.

In Western culture, for many possible reasons, the individual's mind learns to adjust its acceptance of stimuli to both causal systems. It learns that the interrelationships of waking life are stratified and demand specific responses. When it "awakes" in the morning, it observes its position and the surrounding arrangement of things and determines the condition of "waking," adjusting its expectations to a waking causal system. When it begins to dream during sleep the new arrangement of things dictate a reversal of acceptance to a dream causal system. It is not aware of its position in time and space and does not normally distinguish between the experience and waking life. It responds to the dream with many alternatives of action depending on the dream organization. Behavior is flexible,

False awakenings occur when a person dreams that he wakes up in bed and the imagination attempts to reproduce the scene to match the waking expectations of the person. Unfortunately, many times the memory mixes and matches particulars and its failure to duplicate a waking causal system results in either actual awakening or a lucid determination. Lucid dreams in other cases can develop from ordinary dreams when something occurs in the dream that violates the dream causal system to the extent that the consciousness doubts the validity of the experience. Unlike a false awakening, the violation and the interpretation of the dream are along dream lines of interrelationships, dream expectations.

A simple critical attitude or disbelief in the reality of the experience, however, does not necessarily mean that the consciousness will shift its acceptance of stimuli back to a waking one. It may determine that what is happening is "unreal" but still not be centrally aware of its true position in time and space. It might continue to respond and analyze according to dream causality and sense things in terms of separateness rather than interval, distance and form. In such an event, little of the dream will be remembered later as with normal dreams, because the waking mind will not be able to connect the fluid associations and immeasurable time/space relationships of dream stimuli.

An important question is "How does a dream ever violate its own causal system?" The answer possibly lies in three areas of interest: imaginative, emotional, and conceptual.

While a dream causal system offers large variation in imaginative concoctions and innovations, certain dream compositions may be either too bizarre in nature compared with normal dreams, or by their appearance conflict with an already established interrelationship or impose waking methods of organization. Oliver Fox, Celia Green, Patricia Garfield, myself, and practically all lucid researchers have given examples of the first two of these contingencies. The third possibility of imaginative violation, something causing the imposition of waking methods of organization, is similar in ways to Green's "initiation of analytical thought processes" discussed in Part 3; but while Green confuses "analytical processes" with waking logic (she sees analysis and interpretation as occasional whereas I view it as continuous with different dream and waking function), she does lead to the same conclusion for lucid theory.

The dream example I gave in that section will do to illustrate: A friend and I were walking together after a long period apart and I was feeling very happy to be with him again. Naturally, I did not wonder how we happened to be together but sensed both the separateness of when we were last together and another separateness of a point at which we were reunited. Then he said to me, "Thank you for picking me up at the station this morning." This made me impose a waking sense of time and space into the dream in an attempt to remember an exact image of meeting him. Yet I had no memory of him, the morning, or the station and my failure to resolve the missing time, place, or event caused me to think that I must be dreaming.

In all accounts it becomes apparent the a dream "reality," while being considerably more variable than the waking one, has definite limits and arrangements, and the imagination in its creative course of business occasionally crosses those limits and violates those arrangements.

Many early lucid dreams, as discussed in the paper, result from a highly emotionally charged dream experience such as a recurring nightmare. In other words, the emotional association of some dream stimuli is too extreme and unnatural for the dream world, and thus is interpreted as a violation of reality, which then causes a critical attitude toward the dream by the consciousness.

But emotional intensity is not the only manner that personality affects a conscious response to dream material. The person's own sense of self can also determine whether a dream is acceptable or unacceptable. Thus, personality contributes to the criteria for reality. An instance of this influence comes from an article in the *Sundance Community Dream Journal*, v. 1, by Gregory Sparrow who tells us of a dream he had where he discovered a vase of exquisite beauty. The vase caused him to have lucid awareness because he felt it was too beautiful to be real.

But the vase was his creation! Essentially then, he was questioning his own creativity, his own ability to create a vase so beautiful. Dream stimuli are fundamentally limited by the personality, and the ingredients of a dream world can only be as good as the psyche that creates and interprets them.

A third method by which dream violation occurs is the introduction into mental activity of concepts. A concept is not a factor of causality itself but instead an integral unit of interrelationship, sort of a miniature causal system. We must differentiate between a concept and a waking "law" such as gravitation. A waking law is a verity that applies under certain conditions but which has a conceivable opposite that can be imagined if not experienced. A concept, though, is self contained and has no imaginable opposite. When it becomes a part of cognition, the consciousness perceives causality in terms of the concept and any stimuli that violates the concept becomes therefore inconceivable.

One good and universal example of a concept assimilated into cognition and becoming part of dream perception is the "third Dimension." P.D. Ouspensky explains to us in *Tertium Organum* that in crude perception all objects are seen as two-dimensional. A sphere is seen as an oscillating circle and a cube as flat patterns of parallelograms. To see in three dimensions requires a concept of depth or three-dimensionality. Naturally, all early experiences, dreams included, are seen in flat surfaces; but as a child grows, both his dream world and waking world are perceived through an evolving concept of third-dimensionality, perhaps defined as an absorption by the consciousness of a type of reverse artistic perspective—an interrelationship of lines and surfaces. Once this concept is a part of dream experience, a failure of certain stimuli to be responded to as three-dimensionality might cause a dream violation and critical attitude. For example, once in a dream I tried to pick up a ball but could not; the apparent rounded surfaces kept receding into insubstantial and diaphanous circles. In effect, it was an inconceivable event and caused me to doubt the reality of the entire dream.

Another question might be raised as to how two causal systems would develop or work physiologically. It might be proffered that the systems develop in a hologram manner or possibly instead in a hemispheric or bicameral fashion not unlike the manner of conscious evolution outlined by Julian Jaynes in The Origins of Consciousness.

Yet a more important question addresses itself as to the effect of the preceding theoretical scheme on human behavior, both dream and waking. As far as waking behavior is concerned, the effect of causal systems is no more than conditional, the true loci of personality growth are, of course, feelings and needs; and the fact that the consciousness must adapt its responses each day to the rules and relationships of waking life is not by itself a behavioral determination. Whether or not we can jump off buildings and float away might influence our action on roofs, but it can do little to make us feel loved. There are conditions, however, where maladjustment of the mind to a waking level of acceptance might cause certain symptomatic effects. The failure of a developing consciousness to accept or understand all of the physical and social realities of the waking world might make it retreat into the more flexible acceptance level of dream response, and experience waking life with dream methods of organization—the reverse, in other words, of false awakenings and Senoi behavior. A mild result of this might be chronic daydreaming and the severe symptom, schizophrenic withdrawal.

The cause for such a failure to adjust to waking causality could be either a confusion or insecurity in the former case and a loss of emotional faith in the latter. By this I mean that much of what becomes waking reality does so because of faith in our parents and others. They "order" for us much of what we see and can't see. They tell us that monsters do not exist, that God does, that we are worthwhile in this world, that love is real, that the responses we must make are necessary, that dreams are imaginary, etc. But if for some reason we no longer trust or believe in these people, the interrelationships that they have drawn up for us go out the door with them, and as a consequence we might revert to the more natural dream acceptance of stimuli and respond to waking events with a dream sense of reality and time/space. For all practical purposes, we would appear "crazy" to the outside world.

In dreams, the adaptation of the consciousness to a dream causal system in Western society means that behavior is given larger parameters within which to interact with the imaginative and emotional content of REM sleep. The elasticity of dream association and expectation and the less restrictive time/space sense of separateness enable the behavioral variations accounted for by Freudian, Gestalt, and Jungian psychologists. Similarly, many of the interpretive and symbolist explanations for dream material and response might just as well be explained as modified actions in situations occurring in a system of causality with enlarged possibilities of interrelationship. If in dreams we should walk on water, it must be remembered before allusions are drawn that dream water is not the same thing as natural water.

Whether the Senoi or Western method of conscious adjustment to the variant causal systems of dream and waking worlds is more effective for mental health is not answerable at this time. The question is not even being raised here; neither are other questions regarding the following: a speculative influence of hypothetical genetic/archetypal images in the development of dream causality; the plausibility of contorting physics, philosophy, and psychophysics into an approach toward the understanding of precognitive elements in dreams; the conjecturable existence of other causal systems or subsystems accompanying states of mind other than waking and dreaming, e.g. meditative conditions, drug experiences, role organizations, neurotic sensory arrangements, NKEM sleep-thought influences.

Whatever the directions that lucid dreams and their theoretical by-products lead us to in the future, the promise of a causal or organizational study of the mind is surely one of the most curious for science and the arts. If indeed we "wander between two worlds" as the poet once wrote, we must learn to study both worlds for their own opportunities rather than just use one for the sake of the other; and the opportunities are many. In fact, I take a rather minor one now to step out of this discussion and leave only a small story behind. It has been said that once there was an author of books that would write exceedingly long forewords and afterwords, and somewhere between them inject a few lines of the primary treatise. It was believed that the author really had nothing to say but only liked to comment on what he didn't say.

Oh well.

June, 1977

REFERENCES

Adler, A., *What Life Should Mean to You* (Orig, pub. 1933) New York: Capricorn, 1958.

Adrian, E.D., The Activity of Nerve Fibers., Nobel Lecture, Dec. 12, 1932.

Aserinkly, E.and KUftman, N., Regularly Occurring Periods of Eye Motility and Concomitant Phenomena, During Sleep., *Science*, 1955, 118; 273-274.

Bennet, E.L., Diamond, M.C., Krech, D. Rosenaueig, M.R., Chemical and Anatomical Plasticity of Brain. *Science*, 146 ;610, 1964.

Berger, R.J., Experimental Modification of Dream Content by Meaningful Verbal Stimuli. *Brit. J. Psychiat.*, 1963; 109; 722-740.

Bexton, W.H., Heron, W., Scott, T.H., Effects of Decreased Variation in Sensory Environment. *Canada J. Psychol*, 1954, 8:70-76.

Brattgard, S.O., *Acta Radial. Suppl.* 1952, 96, 1.

Bremer, F., Cerebral and Cerebellar Potentials. *Physiol. Rev.*, ; 1958, 38:357.

Broadbent, D.E., Heron, A., *Brit J. Psychol*, 1962, 53:189.

Brush, E., Observations on the Temporal Judgement During Sleep. *Amer. J. Psychiat.*, 1930, 42: 408-411.

Chentsov, I.S., Boroviagin, V.L., Brodskii, V.I., *Biophysica*, 1961, 6:61.

Clark, R.W., *Einstein: The Life and Times*, New York, Avon (1971)

Cone, J.L., *The Postnatal Development of the Human Cerebral Cortex* (Harvard Univ. Press, Cambridge, 1939) 1:104

Cronholm, B., Mellander, L., *Acta Psychiat.*, 1959, 3:18–1957, 32:280.

Delage, Y., *Le Rene*, Les Presses Universitaires de France, Paris, 1919.

Dement, W., The Effect of Dream Deprivation, *Science*,1960, 131:1705-1707.

Dement, W., Wolpert, E.A., The Relation of Eye Movement, Body Motility, and External Stimuli to Dream Content. *Journal Of Exp. P*sychol., 1958, 55:543-553.

Dingman, W.? Sporn, M.B., The Incorporation of 8-A2 guanine into rat brain RNA and its Effect on Maze-learning by the Rat; An Inquiry into the Biochemical Basis of Memory. *J. Psy*chiat. Res., 1961, 1:1

Douglas, R.J., The Hippocampus Behavior. *Psychol. Bull.*, 1967, 67:416-442. van Eeden, F., *A Study of Dreams.* Proceedings of the Society for Psychical Research, 1913, 26:431-461.

Elder, J.A., A Study of the Ability to Awaken at Assigned hours.—/*Psychol. Bull.*, 1941, 38:393.

Evarts, E.V., J. *Neurophysiol.*, 1962, 25:812.

Evarts, E.V., *Progress in Brain Rese*arch, 1965, v.18.

Fantz, R.L., The Origin of Form Perception. *Scientific Am.*, May, 1961.

Feinberg, I. et. al., Sleep Electroencephelographic and Eye Movement Patterns in Schizophrenic Patients. Camp. *Psychiat*, 1964, 5:44-53.

Fisher, C., Dement, W.C., Studies on the Psychopathology of Sleep and Dreams. Am. J. *Psychiat*, 1963, 119:1160-1168.

Fishman, Roffwarg, H., *Psycol. Abstracts*, v. 49, Jan-March, 1973.

Flexnor, L.B., Flexner, J.B.? Roberts, R.B., Memory in Mice Analyzed with Antibiotics. *Science*, 1967, 155:1377.

Flexner, J.B., Flexner, L.B., Stellar, E., *Science*, 1963, 141:57.

Fox, O., *Astral Projection*, Univ. Books Inc. New York, 1962.

Fox, O., The Pineal Doorway. *Occult Review*, 1920.

Fox, 0.;, Beyond the Pineal Door. *Occult Review*, 1920.

Fong, P., Paper read at Am. Phys. Soc., April, 1969.

Foulkes, D. Theories of Dream Formation and Recent Studies of Sleep Consciousness. *Psychol. Bull.*, 1964, 62:236-247.

Foulkes, D., Dream Reports From Different Stages of Sleep. *Journal of Abnormal Psychol.*, 1962, 65:14-25.

Foulkes, D., *The Psychology of Sleep*. New York: Charles Scribner's Sons, 1966.

Freud, S., *The Interpretation of Dreams*, (Orig. pub. 1900) New York: Basic Books, 1956.

Frobenius, K., *Gen Psychol*,1927, 103:100-110.

Fromm, E., *The Forgotten Language* (Orig, pub. 1951) New York: Grove Press, 1957.

Giora, Z., *Am. J. of Psychiat*, 1972.

Graveline, D.E., Balke, B., McKenzie, RE, Hartmen, B., Psycho-biologic Effects of Water-immersion-induced Hypodynamics, *Aerospace Med.*, 1961, 32-387-400.

Green, C.E., *Lucid Dreams*, London: Hamish Hamilton, 1968 (for the Institute of Psychophysical Research).

Halacy, D.S. Jr., *Mind and Memory: Breakthroughs in the Sciences of the Human Mind*, New York: Harper and Row, 1970.

Hamberger, C., Hyden, H., Cytochemical Changes in the Cochlear Ganglion Caused by Acoustic Stimulation and Trauma. *ACTA* Oto-Laryngologia, Supp. 61, 1945.

Hernandez-Pton, R, Chavez-Ibarra, G. Morgane, P.J., Timo-Iaria, C. Limbic, Cholinergic Pathways Involved in Sleep and Emotional Behavior. Exp. *Neurol.*, 1963, 8:93-111.

Horowitz, M.J., Adams, J.E., Rutkin, B.B., Visual Imagery on Brain Stimulation. *Arch. Gen. Pychiat.* 1968, 19:469-486.

Horowitz, M.J., *Image Formation and Cognition*, New York: Meredith Corp., 1970.

Hyden, H.,Protein Metabolism in the Nerve Cell During Growth and Function. *ACTA* Physiol. Scand., 1943, Suppl. 17.

Hyden, H., IV Int. *Congr. Biothem.* Vienna, Vol III, p-64. Pergamon Press, Oxford, 1959.

Hyden, H., *Macromolecular Specificity and Biological Memory*, p.55, M.I.T. Press, Cambridge, Mass., 1962.

Hyden, H., Egyhazi. E. Changes in RNA Content and Base Compositions in Cortical Neurons of Rats in a Learning Experiment Involving Transfer of Handedness. *Proc. N.A.S.*, 1964, 52:1030.

Hyden, H., Pigon, A., J. *Neurochem*, 1069, 6:57.

Jouvet, M., Telencephalic and Rhonbencephalic Sleep in the Cat. In Ciba Foundation Symposium, *The Nature of Sleep*. Boston: Little Brown and Co., 1961, pp.188-206.

Jouvet, M., Mounier, D., Neurophysiological Mechanisms of Dreaming. *Electroenceph. clin. Neurophysiol.* 1962, 14:424.

Jung, C.G., *Basic Writings of C.G. Jung*, Ed. V. de Lasglo, Random House, 1959.

Kleitman, N., Sleep. *Scientific Am.* Nov., 1952.

Langworthy, O.R., *Contrib Embryo.*, 1933, v. 24:1.

Lashley, K.S., *Brain Mechanisms and Intelligence*, Chicago: u, of Chicago Press, 1929.

Levine, R.P., *Readings from Scientific Am.* Dec 1969.

Li, C. Jasper, H., Henderson, L. Jr. The Effect of Arousal Mechanisms on Various Forms of Abnormality in the Electroencephalogram. *Electroenceph. clin. Neurophysiol.*, 1952, 4:513-526

Lindsley, D.B., Attention, Consciousness, Sleep and Wakefulness. Amer. Physiol. Soc, 1960, 3:1553-1593 (cited by Webb, *Sleep: An Experimental Approach*, 1968).

Luby, E.D., Frohanan, C.E., Grisell, J.L., Lenzo, J.E., Gottlieb, J.S., Sleep Deprivation: Effects on Behavior, Thinking, Motor Performance and Biological Energy Transfer Systems. *Psychosom. Med.*, 1960, 22:182-192.

Luce, Mc Guinty, Segal, *Current Research on Sleep and Dreams*, U.S. Gov. Printing Office, 1966.

Mc Guigon and Fannel, *Psychonomic Science*, 1971.

Morrel, F., *Information Storage in Nerve Cells. Information Storage and Neural Control*, Springfield, 111: C.C. Thomas, 1963.

Muldoon, S., *The Projection of the Astral Body*, 1929.

Nissen, H., Chow. K., Semmes, J., *Am. J. Psychol.*, 1951, 6:485.

Omwake, K. Loranz, M., Study of the Ability to Wake at a Specified Time, *J. Appld. Psychol*, 1933, 17-468-474.

Onheiber, P., et al. Sleep and Dream Patterns of Child Schizophrenics. *Arch, of Gen. Psychiat.*, 1965, 12:568-571.

Oswald, I., Falling Asleep Open Eyed During Intense Rhythmic Stimulation. *Brit. Med. J.*, 1960, 1:1450-1455.

Oswald, I., *Sleeping and Waking: Physiology and Psychology*. New York: Elsevier, 1962.

Ouspensky, P.D., On the Study of Dreams and on Hypnotism. C.7, pp. 271-307, in A *New Model of the Universe*, London: Routledge and Hegan Paul, 1960.

Parmelee, A.H., et al. Paper presented to the Association for Psychophysical Study of Sleep. Palo Alto, Calif. March, 1964.

Penfield, W., *Temperal Lobe Epilepsy*, Baldwin, M. and Bailey, P. eds. Springfield, 111. Charles, Thomas, 1958.

Poetzl, 0., The Relationship Between Experimentally Induced Dream Images and Indirect vision. *Psychol. Issues*, 1960, 3:41-120.

Pribram, K.H., Melean, P.D. Neuronogrophic Analysis of Medical and Basal Cerebral Cortex, *Trans. Amer. Nuerol Ass.*, 1960, 85:80-84

Rechtschaffen, A., Discussion of Dr. William Dement's paper. M. Masserman, J.H. ed. *Science and Psychoanalysis* v.7 New York: Grune and Stratton, 1964, pp. 162-170

Rechtschaffen, A. Verdone, P. Wheaton, J. Reports of Mental Activity during Sleep, *Can. Psychiat. Ass. J.* 1963, 8:409-414

Rechtschaffen, A. Vogel, G. Shaikum, G. Interrelatedness of Mental Activity during sleep, *Arch, of Gen. Psychiat*, 1963, 9:537-547

Renneker, R. Presleep Mechanisms of Dream Control. *Psychoanal, Quart.*, 1952, 21:538-536

Richter, D. *Aspects of Learning and Memory*, N.Y. Basic Books, 1966

Roffwarg, H.P., Musia, J.N., Detriment, W.C., Ontogenetic development of the Human Sleep-Dream Cycle. *Science*, 1966, 152:604-619

Roffward, et al., Dream Imagery: Relationship to Rapid Eye Movements of Sleep. *Arch. Gen., Psychiat*, 1962, 7:235

Rosenweig, M.R. Bennet, E.L. Krech, D. *J. Comp. Physiol, Psychol* 1964, 57:438 de Sainte-Denys, H. *Les Reves et les Mayens de les Dinger*. Paris, 1964

Singer, J. *Daydreaming*, Ney York: Random House, 1966

Smith, S. *Out of the Body Experiences*, 1968

Snyder, F. Sleep and Dreaming: Progress in the new Biology of Dreaming. *Am. J. of Psychiat.*, 1965, 122.377-391

Stevens, L.A. *Explorers of the Brain*, N.Y., Alfred Knopf, 1971.

Stoyva, J.M. Post-hypnotically suggested Dreams and the Sleep Cycle. *Arch. Gen. Psychist.*, 1965, 12:287-294

Tart, C. ed. *Altered Stares of Consciousness: A Book of Readings*, New York: John Wiley and Sons Inc, 1969

Tart, C. Effects of Posthypnotic suggestion on the process of Dreaming. Unpub. P.H.D. Dissertation, Univ. of N.C., 1963Tart, C. Hypnotic Suggestion as a Technique for the Control of Dreaming. Paper read at Am. Psychol. Ass., L.A., 1964

Tart, C. Toward the Experimental Control of Dreaming: A review of the Literature. *Psychol. Bull.*, 1965, 64:81-91

Webb, W. *Sleep: An Experimental Approach.* London: Macmillan Co., 1968

Whiteman, J.H.M. *The Mystical Life.* London: Farber and Farber, 1961

Whitman, R.M., Pierce, CM., Maas J. Drugs and Dreams, in Uhr, L., and Miller, J.6., (eds.) *Drugs and Behavior*, New York-John Wiley and Sons Inc., 1960, pp. 591-595

Williams, H.L. Morlock, H.C., Morlock, J.V., Instrumental Behavior During Sleep. *Psychophysiology*, 1966, 2:208-216

Wolpert, E.A., Studies in the Psychophsiology of Dreams II. *Arch, of Gen. Psychiat.*, 1960, 2:231-241.

Wolpert, E.A., Frossman, H. Studies in Psychophysiology of Dreams. I. *Arch, of Neural, and Psychiat.*, 1958, 79:603.

Wolstenholme, G.E.N. *The Nature of Sleep*, (Ciba Fornd. Sym.), Little Brown.

Zinkin, S. Paper read at the B.P.S. Annual Conference, 1965

Ziskind, E., Augsbury, T. Hallucinations in Sensory Deprivation: Method or madness? *Science*, 1965, v. 137.

978-0-595-39539-2
0-595-39539-2